Praise for *Feng Shui For Hawai'i Gardens*

"Fascinating, insightful and full of magic! Clear Englebert's feng shui book is the perfect resource for every gardener in the beautiful Hawaiian Islands."

—Susan Levitt, *Teen Feng Shui* and *Taoist Feng Shui*

"Clear Englebert presents garden feng shui as beautiful as Mother Nature herself. *Feng Shui for Hawai'i Gardens* guides the reader on placement of water features, lighting, statuary and furniture, as well as favorite fragrant, colorful and edible plants that attract the good chi of birds and butterflies. Clear's research provides an excellent resource for all tropical gardening, not just in the Aloha State."

—Jami Lin, founder, Feng Shui Home Study Mastery Program, *Feng Shui Today*

"A book for both feng shui enthusiasts and beginners alike, with loads of tips and great practical ideas. I would recommend *Feng Shui for Hawai'i Gardens* to anyone who wants to create peace and harmony in his or her environment."

—Sarah Bartlett, *Simply Feng Shui* and *Feng Shui for Lovers*

"Filled with practical, easy-to-use recommendations and illustrated with beautiful color photographs, *Feng Shui for Hawai'i Gardens* is the perfect guide for anyone who wants to live and work in a space surrounded by Nature's own beauty. Clear Englebert's extensive knowledge of Hawaiian flora combined with his feng shui expertise will inspire you to surround yourself with healthy, vibrant, lush green chi energies of Mother Nature. This book is definitely an important addition to my library and I will continually refer to it for my feng shui consultations!"

—Master R.D. Chin, feng shui architect, *Feng Shui Revealed*

"This clear, specific how-to guide is certain to help locals and designers make Hawai'i even more visually stunning and energetically sound than it already is. I wish I'd had this book when I was a practicing landscape architect designing hotels in Hawai'i before making feng shui my full-time career."

—Karen Rauch Carter, landscape architect, *Move Your Stuff, Change Your Life*

"Thoughtfully written, magnificently illustrated with color photographs and a great companion for anyone lucky enough to have a garden in Hawai'i. Even if you don't have a Hawaiian garden, you'll want this book for the sheer pleasure of reading it and enjoying its beauty. A must-have for any feng shui or garden devotee!"

—KIRSTEN LAGATREE, *Checklists for Life* and *Feng Shui: Arranging Your Home to Change Your Life*

"With all the books on the subject of feng shui, it is a treat to see a book focused on the unique needs of the Hawaiian Islands and its exotic flora, especially as so much of daily life in a tropical climate is lived outdoors. Clear Englebert has created a book that takes ancient feng shui principles and applies them to many landscaping styles. As one would hope from a book on gardening, this book is beautifully and abundantly illustrated with many useful resources and ideas to guide you every step of the way—so you, too, can transform your outdoors into the relaxing and uplifting sanctuary that you imagined it would be."

—ELLIOT JAY TANZER, *Choose the Best House for You: The Feng Shui Checklist*

"Clear Englebert's *Feng Shui for Hawai'i Gardens* is a lush application of feng shui in tropical latitudes. The plethora of pertinent images, plants, garden settings and diagrams—each worth an easy thousand words—expands the understanding of the positive uses of feng shui with an artistic touch. Those living in more temperate climes will recognize much of the Hawaiian foliage as outdoor transplants or household plants and benefit from learning much about their harmonious placement in their own environments. The feng shui principles, the same everywhere, are simply explained, amply illustrated and presented with serene sense."

—JOHNDENNIS GOVERT, *Feng Shui: Art and Harmony of Place*

FENG SHUI
For Hawai'i
GARDENS

FENG SHUI
For Hawai'i
GARDENS

CLEAR ENGLEBERT

The Flow of Chi Energy in the Tropical Landscape

WATERMARK
PUBLISHING

ISBN 978-1-9356901-5-3

Library of Congress Control Number: 2011941395

Book Design
Leo Gonzalez
Marisa Oshiro

Watermark Publishing
1088 Bishop St., Suite 310
Honolulu, Hawai'i 96813
Telephone 1-808-587-7766
Toll-free 1-866-900-BOOK
sales@bookshawaii.net
www.bookshawaii.net

Printed in China

Contents

Introduction

I'm always charmed by a garden that seems at once an intrinsic part of nature and full of surprises—a space where a combination of a cultured, nurtured living space and the spontaneity of wilderness seems inevitable. Partway through writing this book, I had a conversation with my publisher about the importance of gardens in feng shui. He said, "I wouldn't have thought there was that much to say about what's outside the house." But the interior of a building is a very controlled environment; exteriors are just as important as interiors in feng shui, and once you're outside, *anything* can happen! Many feng shui concerns arise that influence how to landscape, and where and what to plant.

Gardens are important in feng shui because they are your first and best opportunity to do three things:

- Invite good energy into your home
- Balance your home in its surroundings, in relation to other buildings and land features
- Protect your home from harsh or threatening energies.

There is an emphasis in feng shui on the relationship between humans and nature—a call to *notice* nature. Your garden is the opportunity for nature to lure you outside. Its beauty can refresh your spirit as nothing else does. In and of itself, feng shui is not an aesthetic art. An ugly presentation can still be technically correct from a feng shui standpoint. With this book, I hope to guide you in creating a beautiful *and* traditionally correct garden.

Feng shui uses symbolism to establish solutions to less-than-ideal physical situations. For example, plants represent landforms. They can make the home feel snug and nested. But if used incorrectly they can stifle the energy of the home. Feng shui uses a lot of common sense, and you will notice results.

The concept of chi energy is fundamental in understanding feng shui. I hope to make you curious about the energy around *your* home—and to help you understand what you can do to influence that energy. You can think of chi energy as attentive energy. What gets your attention in your garden? The sound, color and movement of birds in a tree will cause you to turn your head. Just as they attract your attention, they attract chi. Other attractors of chi energy are light, fragrance and stunning beauty.

Chi energy can also be thought of as traffic flow. Wind, water, people and animals move around your yard. Where can they move easily? Do the pathways encourage rushing, or do they encourage meandering? Meandering is preferred. A stream that meanders is much more peaceful than a stream that has been unnaturally directed into a straight-line channel.

This book will not delve into the fundamentals of feng shui; rather, its use is to direct you *how* to employ concepts. *Feng Shui for Hawai'i* is the companion to the book you are holding. It covers feng shui basics and is referenced a few times when it covers a topic in depth. I also reference works by other authors I find particularly illuminating; a complete list of suggested titles can be found at the end of this book.

Gardening, like any relationship, requires patience and commitment. I'm an avid gardener myself, and these two mottoes are near and dear to my heart:

"The best fertilizer is the gardener's footprint." There is no substitute for your own chi energy when you work with plants. The more time you spend in your garden, the more you will want to spend time in your garden. It's a very positive cycle. Being out in a garden at dawn is a peaceful and natural start to your day. The good fortune of living in Hawai'i is best appreciated outside in our wonderful varied climate.

"Work with what's working." This is my personal motto inside or outside a home. Outside, it often means that if you have a plant you like and find easy to grow, consider planting more. *Repeat, repeat, repeat* is a professional landscaping rule, and from a feng shui point of view, it maintains serenity. Be aware that serene and boring are not the same—if you find delight in a repeated motif or element, it's certainly not boring!

There are several lists of plants included throughout this book. They are alphabetized by what I feel to be the name most commonly used in Hawai'i. Not every plant is suited to all areas. In fact, some plants I list I advise *against* using.

Please **avoid introducing plants into your neighborhood that will become weeds on neighboring properties or have potential to choke native growth.** It's bad feng shui and bad common sense, but it's often done quite innocently—a gardener is simply unaware a plant has weedy or invasive potential. Plants considered weeds in one part of an island may be difficult to keep alive in a different location on the same island. Some plants, such as autograph tree and night-blooming jasmine, are invasive because the wind and the birds spread them into wilderness areas where the exotic introduced plants overrun the native ones.

If you don't know what plants have weed potential in your area, ask a knowledgeable neighboring gardener or a local nursery who will understand your microclimate. Don't get emotionally attached to a species of plant before knowing something about it—it might be hard to grow in your area, or it might be difficult to control in your area. The Hawaiian Islands have ecosystems more delicate than continental ecosystems. Some plants that once grew easily here are now barely surviving because of introduced pests. Be pono (righteous) and keep these islands well. They were here before we arrived and they'll be here after we're gone. May our time here be one of caring for the land—mālama i ka 'āina.

We live on magnificent islands with a huge variety of plants available. The art of feng shui gardening lies in picking the right plants for your location. Use this book as inspiration; may the information help you to create a garden that makes your heart soar and your life flow. Have fun, and please let me know your results. I would love to see how creative gardeners make use of feng shui principles. ☙

INVITING CHI ENERGY

(The first thing your garden can do for you is to invite good energy onto your property and to your door. A person driving or walking along your road is an example of chi energy. You want heads to turn toward your property as people approach it—and you want them to smile.) *Attracting attention in a positive way is all that's needed, but exuberant beauty is ideal.*

Roadside

Anything that can prick you should not be used along the roadside of your property. (Plants with thorns or dangerous leaves symbolize energy that is threatening or wary.) These plants evolved their protections in response to a harsh environment. They continue to say "harsh." Instead, use plants with round or rounded leaves—friendly plants. They are recommended in most places throughout the home and garden. They are *essential* along the roadside of your property, the driveway and any pathway coming into your property, all the way to your door. (Rounded leaves attract happy, abundant energy. Plants with thorns, spines, barbs, bristles or very sharp stiff leaves (such as yucca or agave) may be quite noticeable, but they're simply not inviting.)

Opposite: The barbs along the leaves of *Aloe arborescens* can easily scratch you. Don't plant them near a pathway.

Top left: Agaves have a very sculptural beauty, but if you fell into them you might end up in the emergency room.

Top right: *Furcraea variegata* is a very striking plant, but you wouldn't want somebody to strike you with it. Don't plant it along the roadside or near your entrance.

Bottom left: New Zealand flax (*Phorium* spp.) is beautiful, but the leaves are too prickly to be near your entrance.

Bottom right: Yucca (*Yucca gloriosa*) is called Spanish bayonet. The leaves resemble swords and do not welcome good energy onto your property.

Left: This *Ptychosperma watanabe* palm does not bring out the tree-hugger in anyone.

Top right: All cycads are poky, and this one is exceptionally so.

Bottom right: It's obvious why *Furcraea variegata* (foreground) and agave (behind) aren't considered friendly plants in feng shui.

There are many plants that have sharp-pointed leaves but pose no danger of injury, such as areca palms (*Dypsis lutescens*). They are not ideal along the roadside or entrance(s) to the property, but since their leaves are floppy they are better than truly dangerous plants. The sword-like appearance of the leaves is a problem: they look as if they could prick you, even if you know they're harmless.

Left: I wouldn't hesitate to shake hands with this graceful areca frond.

Right: Moses-in-the-cradle (also known as oyster plant) is quite snazzy, but don't put it along walkways, driveways or roadsides. The pointed leaves can't really harm you, but they still resemble pāhoa—daggers.

Pucker your face into a tight, prune-like scowl. That's
how the energy looks when it has passed by prickly plants
on its way to your front door. Now break into a big fat smile.
That's how energy finds you when it passes by rounded leaves
on its way to your home. I think of that as "roly-poly Santa
Claus." Happy or harsh—it's as simple as leaf shape.

There are thousands of plants with rounded leaves.
The following lists will get you headed in the right
direction. Rounded-leaf succulents are so numerous they
are catalogued in a special list. Most of them are from the
immense Crassulaceae family, which catalogues 33 genera
and 1,500 species.

**The Crassulacae
family offers a
multitude of options
with round or
rounded leaves.
The frequently
recommended jade
plant belongs in
this family.**

Plant List: Succulents with Round or Rounded Leaves

- **Elephant's Food** (*Portulacaria afra*)—sometimes known as elephant bush, and mistakenly called dwarf jade plant; it's not a true jade plant. It has an intriguing "naturally bonsai" look and can easily be encouraged to have a flowing form, cascading down a tall pot or hillside terrace. 📷 *A1, A2*

- **Fairy Crassula** (*Crassula multicava*)—round-leaf succulents like this can be planted in the ground but also look great in pots where they are upraised and attract more notice. 📷 *B*

- *Hoya kerrii*—a climber.

- **Jade Plant** (*Crassula ovata*)—this plant is the usual feng shui recommendation. It's the most commonly available round-leaf succulent. 📷 *C*

- **Kalanchoe** (*Kalanchoe* spp)—there are many fine kalanchoes, including *K. manginii* and *K. grandiflora*, which is also available with a variegated coloration. 📷 *D*

- **Panda Plant** (*Kalanchoe tomentosa*)—it has furry leaves.

- **Pearly Moonstones** or **Sugar Almond Plant** (*Pachyphytum oviferum*)

- *Peperomia obtusifolia*—there are at least five cultivars, including variegated ones. There are many kinds and sizes, and they all need shade. This one is native to Hawaiʻi. 📷 *E*

- *Peperomia rotundifolia*—this is a creeping or trailing plant. It has tiny leaves and is shade loving.

- *Portulaca oleracae*

- *Portulacaria afra* var. *foliis variegates*

- *Sedum furfuraceum*

- *Sedum globosum*

- *Sedum kamtschataicum*—a ground cover.

- *Sedum sieboldii*—hanging and deciduous.

- *Sedum spathulifolium* 'Cape Blanco'

- **Silver Dollar Plant** (*Crassula arborescens*)

- **Silver Ruffles** or **Silver Crown** (*Cotyledon undulata*)

- **South American Air Plant** or **Aurora Borealis** (*Kalanchoe feltschenkoi variegata*)

- **String-of-Beads** (*Senecio rowleyanus*)—it has trailing stems and looks nice in a tall pot.

A1

A2

B

C

D

E

Plant List: Round- or Rounded-Leaf Plants
See photos pages 14-15

- **'Ākia** (*Wilkstroemia uva-ursi*)—there are about a dozen species of 'ākia, some with rounder leaves that others. Native, lovely and easy to grow, it makes a perfect hedge. 📷 *A1, A2*

- **Autograph Tree** (*Clusia rosea*)—regular or dwarf, it has round leaves but it's too invasive in Hawai'i. Don't plant it. 📷 *B*

- **Bingabing** (*Macaranga grandifolia* or *mappa*)—has huge round leaves but is quite weedy (especially in wet areas), so beware. 📷 *C*

- **Blue Daze** (*Evolvulus glomeratus* subsp. *grandiflorus*)—a common groundcover. It grows well in full sun and does not grow very tall. 📷 *D*

- **Dinnerplate Panax** (*Polyscias scutteleria*)—has glossy leaves that are almost perfectly round and big enough to serve as a plate—hence the name. (📷 *E1, E2*) It is also available with smaller, variegated leaves. 📷 *E3*

- **Eucalyptus** (*Eucalyptus* spp.)—can be kept fairly low. Its round, silvery leaves are quite delightful and refreshingly fragrant. 📷 *F*

- **Galenga-Grass** (*Dichondra micrantha*)—low (one to three inches), and not a true grass; the leaves are nicely rounded. It is also called lawnleaf, because it can be mowed. It's best in wet areas, where it's quite attractive around stepping stones.

- **Kamani** (*Calophyllum inophylum*)—a great substitute for the invasive autograph tree. It has fragrant flowers.

- **Kōpiko** (*Psychotria* spp.)—there are 11 species of this endemic plant. Some have nicely rounded leaves. It has fragrant flowers, but it needs shade and moisture. 📷 *G*

- **Mirror Plant** (*Coprosma repens*)—the leaves are very rounded and shiny; it's sometimes called the varnish plant because of this. 📷 *H*

- **Mistletoe Fig** (*Ficus deltoidea*)—a shrub, not a tall tree. It makes a delightful container plant. 📷 *I*

- **Natal Plum** (*Carissa macrocarpa*)—there are thornless varieties: 'Tomlinson' and 'Boxwood Beauty.' Natal plums are drought tolerant, have fragrant flowers and edible fruit, and can be grown close to the ocean.

- **Naupaka** (*Scaevola taccada*)—the leaves of the mountain naupaka (naupaka kuahiwi, 📷 *J1*) are not rounded. Beach naupaka (naupaka kahakai, 📷 *J2*) is the plant most people are familiar with. It grows easily at lower elevations and has rounded leaves with sap often used to keep goggles from fogging.

Plant List: Round- or Rounded-Leaf Plants

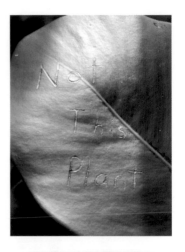

- **'Ōhi'a Lehua** (*Metrosideros polymorpha*)—a much-loved native tree with rounded leaves (📷 *K1*) and beautiful flowers which are usually red (📷 *K2*), but sometimes yellow (📷 *K3*) and occasionally white.

- **Periwinkle** (*Catharanthus roseus*)—cheerful with its year-round blooms, it has the Hawaiian name kīhāpai, and is originally from Madagascar.

- **Pilea**—these low-growing plants are delightful (especially *serpeyllacea*). *P. nummulariifolia* has interestingly textured leaves, as if they were quilted. A warning about *P. microphylla*: it can grow in impossible situations (like cliffsides) but it's extremely weedy. It throws its seeds, earning it the name artillery plant.

- **Pittosporum**—there are several that grow well in Hawai'i, including *Pittosporum hosmeri* (hō'awa), which is endemic. *P. tobira* 'Wheeler's Dwarf' is small enough to make a delightful container plant. All the varieties have rounded leaves and are very easy to grow. Some are *too* easy—*P. pentandrum* and *P. undulatum* are both invasive, so avoid planting them. 📷 *L*

- **Pōhinahina**. (*Vitex rotundifolia*)—for dry areas, this and 'ākia are often the best choices. Its light green leaves are round and welcome good energy. 📷 *M*

- **Pua Kenikeni** (*Fagraea berteroana*)

- **Sea Grape** (*Cocoloba uvifera*)—with nice, thick leaves, it's also available in dwarf forms.

See photos pages 14-15

Some people scratch their initials on the leaves of the autograph tree, but this is what should be written.

A1

A2

B

C

D

E1

E2

E3

F

G

H

I

J1

J2

K1

K2

K3

L

M

There's also a huge category of leaf shape that can be thought of as somewhat rounded. Feel free to use plants with somewhat-rounded leaves anywhere that rounded leaves are recommended. Their energies are quite similar. It's always nice to encourage native plant growth; here are some that do well in dry areas.

Plant List: Native Plants with Somewhat-Rounded Leaves

- **Kulu'ī** (*Nototrichium sandwicense*)—does well in dry areas. The O'ahu variety is quite silvery; *N. divaricatum* grows low and spreads more.

- **'Aiea** (*Nothocestrum* spp.)—the plant for which the town was named.

- **'Āweoweo** (*Chenopodium oahuense*)—the leaves of this shrub are edible. Also called 'āheahea.

- **'Uhaloa** (*Waltheria indica*)—it's rather weedy.

It's fine to have a solid fence or stone wall along the front of the property, but soften its severe look with some plantings on the outside. If the wall is right next to the road or sidewalk, that's unfortunate because it moves energy past your property too quickly. Make that wall interesting—perhaps add epiphytic orchids or ferns into the rock wall.

A

B

C

Plant List: Plants for Rock Walls

- **Christmas Cactus** (*Schlumbergera ×buckleyi*) and Thanksgiving Cactus (*Schlumbergera truncata*)—both are thornless.

- **Epidendrum Orchid**—these orchids don't need much; some dirt and moss in the cracks between rocks is usually enough. 📷 A

- **Laua'e Fern** (*Microsorum scolopendria*)—tends to spread. It is one of many ferns that can grow in a puka in a rock wall. 📷 B

- **Moa** (*Psilotum nudum*)—can almost grow in midair. It can easily grow in the cracks of a rock wall. The word also means "chicken" in Hawaiian. 📷 C

You could also allow some leafy plants (such as monstera or allamanda) to spill over the top of the wall. If home security is a big issue, it becomes your artistic challenge to create an inviting look without hindering visibility. Whatever your situation, the first view should be lush and inviting—even if you are discouraging intruders. Flourishing plants help bring the energy of abundance to your life.

The very front line of your property is not a good place for a deciduous plant which drops its leaves during part of the year. When the plant looks barren and dead, it invites that same energy. Most plumerias are deciduous, but the Singapore varities (*Plumeria obtusa*) are evergreen at lower elevations.

At lower elevations, Singapore plumerias do not lose their leaves, so they never look barren.

Driveway

There's nothing wrong with having a lawn directly against the driveway. But if you have special plantings along the edge of the driveway, the leaves of those plants should be round, not sharp.

Entrance

The first important spot in your garden is where the driveway meets the road. This is your big chance to call out to the world to bring good energy your way. For larger properties, this is the first view that beckons entry into the garden. The power of the first impression cannot be overestimated. For smaller lots, use plantings that are more attractive and noticeable than those used along the front edge of your property.

The place where your driveway (or any pathway) meets the road is the mouth of your property. Give that mouth a bit of lipstick to attract good chi. Put colorful plantings on each side of your driveway (or pathway) where it meets the road. Red is an ideal color at the entrance because it is a strong, noticeable color. Don't color the entire front of your property red—that's not the idea. Because red is so important, it is used very *deliberately* in feng shui.

Stop signs are red to make them noticeable. The color is your way of saying, "Stop, Good Energy, come in *here*." There are many of shades of red; some are so dark, they look

Opposite: A curved driveway slows down chi energy so that it's mellow when it reaches your home.

Below: Use red plants at the entrance of your driveway.

Left: 'Bea's Red' ti is definitely bright enough to attract good energy onto your property.

Right: 'Fire Fountain' ti is appropriately named. This kind of red grabs your eye and doesn't let go.

Left: This ti is quietly beautiful, but visual quiet is not what you want at the entrance to your driveway.

Right: 'Tagami #3' is a very graceful ti, but the color is too dull to be at the entrance of your driveway.

almost black. Don't use a dark, dull red at your entrance—use a plant that has a color with real pizazz. The red color should be visible year-round—so the plants should either blossom throughout the year or have bright red leaves.

There are countless plants that bloom red intermittently, and if you're a talented gardener and relish the challenge, you could have a succession of plantings to ensure year-round red flower color. But most folks want it simple and easy, so they pick from a fairly short list of plants that will reliably produce year-round red flowers. Here are some of your best options:

Plant List: Plants with Red Flowers, Year-Round

- **Anthurium, Red** (*Anthurium xferrierense*)—perfect for a shady location. Anthuriums look exotic yet are easy to grow. 📷*A1, A2*

- **Begonia** (*Begonia* spp.)—dragonwing begonia has red flowers, but subsequent generations might revert to pink. Pentas shares this trait, and you could end up with white flowers if you completely rely on self-seeding for new keiki.

- **Cigar Flower** or **Pua Kīkā** (*Cuphea ignea*)—it's sometimes called firecracker plant, which confuses it with the plant listed below. It is a small bush loaded with red blossoms. 📷 *B*

- **Daylily, Red** (*Hemerocallis* spp.)—individual flowers last only a day, but in any given clump, at least one new flower will be in bloom every day. The Hawaiian name is līlia pala'ai. 📷*C*

- **Firecracker** (*Russelia equisetiformis*)—the flowers are small but abundant. It's excellent for slopes. 📷 *D*

- **Flame Violet** (*Episcia cupreata*)—this delightful little groundcover is good for shady locations. It has red flowers and variegated leaves, both quite attention getting. 📷*E*

- **Geranium** (*Pelargonium* spp.)—they may seem a bit old fashioned, but they can say "home" in a very authentic way. Plus, they are so easy to grow!

continued on next page

A1 A2 B

C D E

Plant List: Plants with Red Flowers, Year-Round
continued

- **Hearts-and-Flowers** (*Aptenia cordifolia*)—since this is an iceplant, it can tolerate almost any condition and continue to thrive. It's an excellent groundcover for full-sun locations. 📷 *F*

- **Hibiscus** (*Hibiscus* spp.)—the large blossoms look tropical year-round. (📷 *G*) Some, like the Turk's cap (*Malvaviscus penduliflorus*), aren't troubled by the mites that cause disfigured, bumpy leaves. The Turk's cap is sometimes called the firecracker hibiscus; for pūpū you can use a pastry bag to fill the inside of the edible flowers with soft cheese or pâté.

- **Impatiens** (*Impatiens* spp.)—beautiful if watered sufficiently. *Impatiens walllerana* is the more weedy species, but it's sometimes more reliable for year-round red flowers, depending on the location. *Impatiens hawkeri* is a species from New Guinea. 📷 *H*

- **Jatropha** (*Jatropha itegerrima*)—a small tree that always has red flowers. It does fine in dry conditions, but without pruning, it becomes straggly. 📷 *I1, I2*

- **Pentas** (**Pentas lanceolata**)—this low-maintenance plant attracts butterflies. It grows about three feet high and sprawls a bit, but not badly. It doesn't have a particularly "tropical" appearance but has my highest recommendation for ease of cultivation. 📷 *J*

F G H

I1 I2 J

CRED

THE IMPORTANCE OF THE COLOR RED IS CROSS-CULTURAL. LOOK
AT HOW MANY FLAGS INCORPORATE RED INTO THEIR DESIGN.
RED, ALONG WITH YELLOW, WAS THE MOST IMPORTANT COLOR
IN OLD HAWAI'I. RED IS VERY IMPORTANT IN CHINESE CULTURE.
THERE ARE OVER 100 WORDS FOR "RED" IN MAORI. IN ALL
LANGUAGES, WITH NO EXCEPTION, RED IS THE EARLIEST COLOR
TERM TO APPEAR.

AKA—JAPANESE
HONG—CHINESE
MÀU DO—VIETNAMESE
MERAH—INDONESIAN
MUMU—SAMOAN
NYEKUNDU—SWAHILI
PAHLGA̋HN—KOREAN
PIROS—HUNGARIAN
PULA—TAGALOG
PUNAINEN—FINNISH
PUNANE—ESTONIAN

ROJO—SPANISH
ROOD—DUTCH
ROSSO—ITALIAN
ROT—GERMAN
ROUGE—FRENCH
RUBER—LATIN
RUDHIRA—SANSKRIT
'ULA—HAWAIIAN
URA—TAHITIAN
VERMELHO—PORTUGUESE
VERMELL—CATALAN

Above is the Chinese
character for "red."

Above is the Japanese
character for "red."

Left: The brilliant red
of this amaryllis lies
hidden underground
in a bulb for most of
the year.

Right: During its
blooming season,
red jade vine is
spectacular.

Top: Green mangoes blend in with the background foliage even when seen close up.

Bottom: Once a mango has turned red, you can easily spot it from a distance. The red catches your eye and attracts chi energy.

MANGOES

MANGOES ARE A GOOD EXAMPLE OF THE POWER OF RED (AND YELLOW). WHILE MANGOES ARE GREEN, WE DON'T MUCH NOTICE THEM—BUT ONCE THEY TURN TO YELLOW AND RED, WE CAN'T STOP OUR EYES FROM BEING DRAWN TOWARD THEM.

Crown of thorns has beautiful bright flowers *(inset)*, but its severe thorns make it inappropriate near a driveway or entrance.

These plants bloom *almost* all year:

Plant List: Additional Plants with Red Flowers

· **Chinese Hat Plant** (*Holmslioldia sanguinea*)—has a very long season of flowering, but not quite year-round. The cultivar 'Lipstick' seems to have the brightest red. 📷 *A*

· **Desert Rose** (*Adenium obesum*)—never loses all of its leaves, and when it blooms, heads turn. "Obesum" in the name refers to the fat root. 📷 *B*

· **Ginger, Red** or **'Awapuhi 'Ula'ula** (*Alpinia purpurata*)—has a much longer blooming season than other gingers and can bear flowers nearly all year in certain areas. It's also available in dwarf varieties. 📷 *C*

· **Ixora** (*Ixora casei*)—has a very neat appearance and is available with true red flowers. 'Super King' has intensely red flowers that are truly king-size. 📷 *D*

A

B

C

D

A very tropical and easy way to add red at the entrance of your property is with red-leaf plants. Croton and red ti are the two most obvious choices for bold, colorful leaves. Their leaves are often a mix of colors, depending on the variety and the age of the individual leaf. The age of the leaf makes a big difference in croton color, but it doesn't always affect red ti color. There are varieties of ti with leaves that stay bright red and never turn green even when they age, such as 'Lilinoe.' Some ti have brilliant red leaves with no white, such as 'Red Sister' and 'Red & Black.' For a wider (more oblate) leaf try a 'Red Juno.' Do some shopping around when buying red ti—you're going to be seeing it for a while, so pick something you really like!

Hilo holly (*Ardisia crenata*) thrives in the shade and has lovely red berries. It's not a true holly (which is in the genus *Ilex*), and although the leaves bear a resemblance, they are not sharp and prickly like real holly. Remember that colorful plants for the entry must not be thorny, so bougainvillea should not be used. Even the so-called "thornless" varieties of bougainvillea have blunted thorns— still considered problematic from a feng shui point of view.

If everyone in a neighborhood used *exactly* the same kind of plant at the mouth of their driveway, the effect would be diminished. Creativity is needed to make your driveway distinct and attractive.

The color at the driveway doesn't *have* to be red. It can be any very noticeable color that is not repeated along the front of your property. Yellow is a good second choice. The idea is to draw visual energy right to your driveway.

Plant List: Plants with Red Leaves

- **Acalypha** (*Acalypha godseffiana*)—from a distance, it looks almost like a cut-leaf maple. 📷*A*

- **Caladium** or **Kalo Kalakoa** (*Caladuim bicolor*)—has interesting variegations which often include red. These varieties are very red: 'Red Flash,' 'Firecracker Red' and 'Florida Red Ruffles.' 'Thai Red' is more pink, but it's extremely noticeable. 📷*B*

- **Coleus** (*Solenostemon scutellarioides*)—can provide a very brilliant red but needs adequate moisture to look its best. Don't plant the dark purple or rusty colors at an entrance. There are some very fiery red coleus varieties, such as 'Flamingo,' 'Forest Fire,' and 'Stella Red.' 'Rubaiyat' has a slight purple blush, giving it a striking magenta color. 📷*C*

- **Croton** (*Codiaeum variegatum pictum*)

- **Dragonwing Begonia** (*Begonia* spp.) 📷*D*

- **Iresine** (*Iresine herbstii*)—does well in sun or shade and is surprisingly hardy for such a delicate-looking plant. When the sun shines, it can be quite mesmerizing. Like begonias, it roots easily from cuttings. 📷*E*

- **Joyweed** (*Alternanthera tenella*)—there are many varieties of this groundcover. It grows like a weed and is a joy to behold. It stays fairly low and tolerates dry conditions well. 📷*F*

- **Ti, Red** (*Cordyline terminalis*)

A   B   C

D   E   F

If your house is hidden from the road by plants or a fence, you are under an even greater obligation to make your driveway entrance stand out visually. There's a bit of disagreement about whether or not it's okay to have the front enclosure—fences, walls, hedges—totally hide the house from the street. The main concern is that unless the front enclosure is low enough to see over, the people in the home could feel penned in.

Some people in rural areas have security concerns about noticeable driveway entrances. They don't want to attract the wrong sort of people to their driveway, so they want a nothing little driveway—"No fancy house at the end of this driveway!" I understand that, but it doesn't change things. You get what you ask for. Ask for a little more than nothing—make your driveway entrance at least a little more attractive. And *deal with your home security*! If your house is not secure, it could be targeted for burglary no matter what your driveway or garden looks like. Feng shui is not a substitute for a lock.

Bunching bamboo is a very manageable plant. If it gets too tall, just cut it.

PRIVACY

IF YOU WANT PRIVACY IN YOUR FRONT YARD, THE BEST WAY TO DO IT IS TO MAKE THE ENCLOSURE (FENCE OR HEDGE) AS HIGH AS IT NEEDS TO BE BUT NO HIGHER. A THICK BUNCHING BAMBOO COULD BE PERFECT, BECAUSE (BEING A GRASS) IT CAN BE CUT DOWN SEVERELY AND STILL RECOVER. SOME PLANTS TAKE WELL TO TRIMMING AND SOME DON'T—I'VE SEEN SOMEONE (WHO DIDN'T KNOW BETTER) CUT OFF THE TOPS OF RHAPIS PALMS, THINKING THEY WOULD GROW BACK LIKE CORNSTALK DRACAENA OR TI. A DEAD RHAPIS PALM IS NOT A THING OF BEAUTY! BE ADVISED: YOU CAN'T CUT THE TOP OFF A PALM TREE AND EXPECT IT TO LIVE.

Gates and Fences

A gate must be secure—otherwise, why bother? A gate with good feng shui can attract positive energy. One imagines there must be something very nice behind such a fine gate.

A gate should either slide open or swing inward. If a gate swings outward, it repels energy (and can damage vehicles). If a gate *must* open out, say so on the gate and brightly mark where a vehicle should safely stop.

Plain gates are fine, but neither gates nor fences should have spiky points (like spears) on top. If the spikes have balls on top of each point, that is fine in feng shui. Water imagery on gates can symbolize water (representing money) flowing *away* from your home—not good. This includes gates with sealife designs or a wavy shape. If your home has that kind of gate and you don't want to change it, put a mirror on the house, facing the gate, and say out loud that your intention is to *pull* the good fortune back up into the house. Don't paint a wavy gate red; it symbolizes conflict—fire and water.

Neither gates nor fences (nor brick walls for that matter) should have a herringbone pattern. That's called "reverse fortune." It's not so bad in a pathway, but as a vertical pattern, it signals that things are going up and then they're going down. If your gate or fence has a herringbone pattern, plant a vine to obscure it, perhaps pakalana (*Telosma cordata*) for its heavenly fragrance.

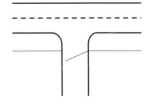

A gate should swing into the property.

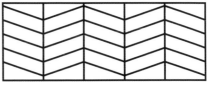

A herringbone pattern is called "reverse fortune" and is not recommended.

What a happy gate! I've seen more expensive gates, but I've never seen one that made me smile more. A perfect feng shui gate—it even has red.

If you want to use Compass Feng Shui when designing your gate, I recommend *Feng Shui Dos and Taboos: A Guide to What to Place Where* by Angi Ma Wong (Pacific Heritage Books, December 2000). It has very clear instructions.

Opposing Driveways

When two driveways are *directly* across the road from each other, they are in competition for luring chi energy. The larger one usually wins— it's as simple as that.

You can increase the size of your driveway, but I prefer to make it more noticeable. Use plants or ornamentation to make your driveway entrance extravagantly stunning. Heads should turn toward *your* driveway. Use bright or noticeable sculpture, pottery or plants (but remember, no spiky-leaf or thorny plants). Lovely pavement on the driveway surface could remedy this situation very well. Even an arresting mailbox would work.

This driveway provides necessary traction while still allowing the earth to breathe.

Driveway Surface

Driveways made of asphalt or cement are not ideal because they are considered to block energy rising from the earth. If cement is used it can be dyed the same color as the surroundings, which helps to alleviate the problem. If the cement develops accidental cracks, it should be patched—or use red to symbolically repair the cracks. Put a tiny drop of red paint (nail polish works) discreetly down in each crack. As you do, say out loud, "You're fixed." Some driveways consist of two paved strips for the tires. These are never a problem, since the middle is open to the earth and can be planted with grass or a ground cover. They are a good solution for steep driveways. Page 25 of *Feng Shui for Hawai'i* deals with the topic of bumpy driveways—basically, fix them if you can. If not, please refer to the other book.

The first part of the driveway is called the apron. It should splay out where it meets the road, symbolizing the funneling of good energy into your life. There's usually a straight-line indentation (a purposeful crack) where the apron meets the rest of the driveway. In wet areas that straight crack can support a surprisingly healthy line of green grass. The green contrasts strongly with the cement and therefore represents a cutting-off energy. Either kill that green line of grass (hot water is an effective non-toxic method) or put a line of red "something" connecting the apron cement and the rest of the driveway cement. The "something" could be red nail polish or red paint, used very discreetly—it could even be a red paperclip.

A driveway that splays open at the road funnels good energy into the property.

Gravel is better than asphalt or cement, especially for flat driveways. But if gravel isn't your style, consider zoysia grass. Zoysia is very tolerant of being driven on. It is low-maintenance, once established,

and 'Emerald' zoysia is particularly excellent. There is an exquisite tiny variety called temple grass (*Zoysia matrella*), but it's too lovely to drive on. It's undoubtedly the most beautiful of all lawn grasses; however, it is expensive.

I've seen driveway surfaces in Hawai'i made of crushed glass. These are not advisable; the symbolism is that things are broken. And since it's the first thing seen as you enter the property, this message cannot be missed. If you want a sparkly driveway or sidewalk, use mica in the cement mix.

Driveway Slope

The ideal driveway is fairly level where it meets the road. A driveway should not slope steeply uphill or downhill at that point.

A steep slope uphill from the road suggests that energy

Above: Gravel driveways may seem humble, but humble is not bad in feng shui.

Above left: It's hard to resist going barefoot on temple grass. It looks so inviting.

coming to the house gets tired and rolls back out before reaching the house. For driveways that slope steeply uphill, put a small mirror in a discreet location at the beginning of the driveway, reflecting up toward the house. Its purpose is to reflect back energy that would otherwise roll out to the road. Silver reflecting balls also work. If possible, create a hump like a speed bump in your driveway, near where it meets the road. Put it far enough back from the road so that it isn't awkward to come and go from your driveway.

A steep slope downhill from the road says that life could be an uphill struggle for you when you leave your house. A steep downhill driveway should be made light and bright, to lift the energy that has to trudge up to the road. Use plants with the brightest colors of red and yellow, as well as white. Solar lights that glow gently along the driveway are another way to lift energy.

Driveway Shape

A short straight driveway is not a problem. If the driveway is longer, it should curve gracefully.

Long straight driveways often happen in Hawai'i because of "flag lots," which usually have straight, narrow driveway easements. That kind of driveway is not desirable in feng shui because it conducts energy too quickly. It's not so bad if the line of the driveway misses the house, but if there are rooms of the house directly in line with the driveway, put a small mirror on the house about the same height as the headlights of a car. It symbolizes the energy of the straight line reflecting away from your home. It's a good idea to say this when you put the mirror in place.

To slow the energy speeding along a long straight driveway, don't use an edger to make a distinct line. Instead, try to obscure the edge of the driveway by planting something like hearts-and-flowers, joyweed or purple wandering Jew along the side of the road.

Left: This driveway does not aim at the house.

Right: This driveway aims at the house. Put a mirror facing the driveway to reflect energy.

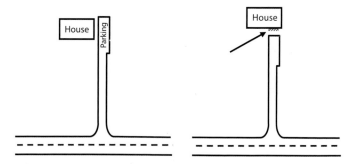

If there's enough room, plant some *very interesting* specimen plants at intervals alongside the driveway. Make that straight line drive a very memorable one—that will truly slow energy down. *See also: Chapter 3, "T-Intersection," pages 79-80.*

Plant stunning flowers, such as heliconia, beside a long straight driveway.

D-shaped driveways are seen differently by various feng shui consultants. I tend to be of the school that says, "D equals divorce." My experience as a consultant tells me that homes with D-shaped driveways tend to be places where good relationship energy is elusive— sometimes divorce, sometimes just staying single. Being on the convex side of a curved road is bad enough, but it seems much worse when the offending road is your own driveway on your own property.

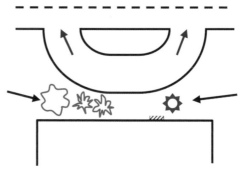

If you're living in a home with a D-shaped driveway *and* having relationship problems, I highly recommend these cures:

I advise against a D-shaped driveway. It signifies going separate ways. If you do have one, put plants and a crystal or mirror between the driveway and house.

• Put a crystal between your driveway and your home. It can be small—the size of a rosary or ojuzu bead. Put it down low somewhere and, if need be, use glue so it will stay. Say out loud something like, "This crystal symbolizes dispersing any harsh energy of the driveway (or the cars on it) before it reaches my peaceful home."

• Put a very small mirror on the house, down low (or on the side of the curb, between the driveway and the house), the shiny side of the mirror toward the driveway. Say something like, "This mirror symbolizes reflecting away any harsh energy of the driveway (or the cars on it) before it reaches my peaceful home."

• Any vegetation between the D-shaped driveway and the house should be extravagantly thick and at least as high as standard headlights, if not big truck headlights. The plants serve as a buffer between the home and the outward curve of the driveway. Fullness is the main thing—think monstera.

Monstera works well to buffer the problematic energy of a D-shaped driveway.

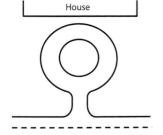

House

A circle driveway is not a problem.

Circle drives are fine in feng shui, as long as there is only one driveway entrance at the road.

Parking

The approach to the garage or carport is in some ways as important as the approach to the front door. It is sometimes used more than the front door, and use accounts for a lot in feng shui. Rounded-leaf plants should be used around the parking area and on the way to the front door. Avoid vast expanses of pavement or gravel, especially near the house. They look barren because they *are* barren. If the pavement must be there, perhaps it could be textured like cobblestones. Even better, install a paving system that allows grass to grow. *See Resources, Permeable Paving, page 194.*

If you already have a large expanse of cement pavement, balance it with some extravagantly lush plantings (such as heliconia or monstera) at the edge of the pavement.

Separate garages or carports are preferred in feng shui. That way the car fumes stay away from the residence. The old-style Hawai'i homes were always built with a separate garage, back when cars were first coming into common use here. If your garage is under the same roofline as your house, don't back the car into your garage. The exhaust pipe should be near the garage door, not near the interior of the house, where it would be symbolically passing gas at the house. In general, don't keep the car pointed out toward the street—that symbolizes the wish to drive away and not linger at home. If cars are often parked so the headlights are aimed at rooms of the house, put a little mirror on the house facing the car. The mirror should be placed at the height of the headlights. The use of the mirror is especially important if the vehicle aims at a bedroom. Some garages are never used for cars—they are used for living or storage space, and the cars are parked in the driveway. This may not be the most aesthetic arrangement, but it poses no feng shui problems.

Above: This type of paving system is ideal because there's plenty of traction, yet the energies of the earth and the atmosphere can interact.

Left: This sign is painted in traditional Hawaiian colors and is quite noticeable. There is no doubt about where to park!

Guest parking should be obvious or plainly marked. If it's not, some good chi energy is missing you. If you're in doubt about whether or not the guest parking is obvious, then it's probably not obvious to someone just arriving at your home. Sometimes the best option is to use signs. The advantage of using signs is that they leave no doubt, and if signage is done nicely, it can actually enhance the landscape.

Near the Door

If a ***walkway*** leads to the front door from the sidewalk, it should not be long and straight and aim right at the front door. The best thing is to create a walk that gently meanders. If you can't take up the cement and redo it, let some plant leaves cross over the edge of the cement so that what's seen isn't a long straight line. Do not use an edger on a long straight walkway. When working with a narrow space like a walkway, it's important to

This graceful walkway would be too narrow if it led to the front door. Placed beside the home, as this one is, it adds much charm.

Opposite: Even a short walkway benefits from a curve—the home seems more gracious and welcoming.

know the difference between "meandering" and "pinching" plantings. Meandering plantings zigzag across the two sides of the walkway. Pinching plantings are positioned directly across from each other. Ideally, a person walking along your walkway after a rain should not get wet from brushing against leaves.

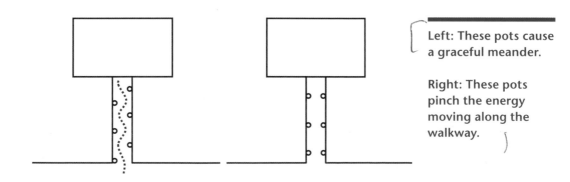

Left: These pots cause a graceful meander.

Right: These pots pinch the energy moving along the walkway.

Walkways that splay out where they meet the common sidewalk are considered to funnel more good fortune to your house. However, the exception is a long, straight walkway that aims at the front door. The walkway would be pulling in even more energy to slam into the front door. Don't use trees to line a long, straight walkway to the front door. This is sometimes done with palms, but it only increases harsh energy.

Left: A long, straight walkway directs energy too forcefully at a front door; a splay at the beginning only compounds the problem.

Middle: Curves in a long walkway with a splay help slow energy.

Right: Lining a straight walkway with trees also increases harsh energy aimed at the door.

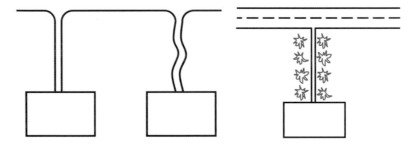

An interesting pattern in a zig-zag arrangement causes fast energy to slow down along this walkway.

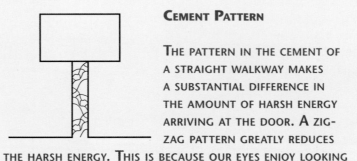

CEMENT PATTERN

THE PATTERN IN THE CEMENT OF A STRAIGHT WALKWAY MAKES A SUBSTANTIAL DIFFERENCE IN THE AMOUNT OF HARSH ENERGY ARRIVING AT THE DOOR. A ZIG-ZAG PATTERN GREATLY REDUCES THE HARSH ENERGY. THIS IS BECAUSE OUR EYES ENJOY LOOKING AT THE PATTERN AND THEREFORE LINGER. FEW EYES WANT TO LINGER ON A PLAIN, GRAY SIDEWALK. LET YOUR IMAGINATION HAVE FUN WITH THIS.

Ming Tang

The area outside the front door is the ming tang—"bright hall." The area just inside a front door is the interior ming tang (discussed on page 83 of *Feng Shui for Hawai'i*). The exterior ming tang is more important because of the huge influence it has on the energy that's just about to enter your life. It's a crucial area because the front door is the *mouth* of your home. It is as important as the mouth of your property. **Plants must never obscure the front door.** Instead, they should accentuate it. Also, they should be balanced around it. A formal symmetrical balance, with matching plants on each side of the door, is often ideal. If that would be an attractive presentation for your home, I highly recommend it. It's appropriate to go for the gusto here—the more attention your front door gets, the better.

(The front door should be immediately noticeable when you arrive at the house. A prominent front door ensures that energy will find you. The reason some people paint front doors red in feng shui is to draw attention. If the door is already noticeable, there is little or no need for that.)

If the front door area doesn't lend itself to the formality of a color repeated on both sides, then use any bright color near the door. The bright color mostly has to say, "Look here—notice this." Absolutely any color can work so long as it stands out. Red is a traditional, but not always the perfect, choice. The noticeable color can come from a plant (leaf or flower) or a planter. Using a container as the source of an eye-catching color means that you can use an easy-care plant in the pot. Make sure its leaves are round, because it's near the mouth of the house. I often recommend common succulents such as jade plant. It's available in 'Tricolor' and 'Variegata' as well as the more common all-green. Not only are the leaves invitingly round, they are also thick and juicy. That symbolizes abundance. *See Plant List: Succulents with Round or Rounded Leaves, page 10.*

As mentioned before, a common way to energize a front door is to paint it red, or any very noticeable color, on the outside. That particular color should not be repeated in paint

Right: These red stairs are quite striking with the blue house and leave no doubt as to where to go. Empty pots near the front door are not a good idea, however. Add umbrellas or a jade plant.

Left: Jade plant is a perfect choice near the front door because the leaves are rounded and approachable.

on the front of the house, because the idea is to make it stand out. If the front door is a beautiful stained wood, I do not recommend painting it unless it is a very hidden door. Instead, use a very bright color (such as red or yellow) on each side of the door, drawing attention to the mouth of the home. An example of this is to paint the trim of the door a very bright color. If you use a brown primer first, you won't have to use as many coats of red to get good coverage. Don't paint your front door red if you leave it open frequently for air circulation. Put the red on the outside of the screen door instead. A red pot near the entrance is also a good way to

A brilliant red pot near the front door is an excellent way to pull good energy to your home. The leaves of this rhapis palm look as if they're ready to shake your hand and say, "Howdy."

make the door area noticeable.

Another way to bring attention to a door is to flank it with objects on either side to center the door within a defined space. Flanking is the beginning of framing, and framing is a powerful attention-getter. Flanking can be done with pots of plants or small shrubs, but be sure that the leaves and branches don't touch the house. Yellow pottery may look more appealing than red with bungalow-style homes.

A hidden front door suggests that energy will have a hard time finding you. I once arrived at a client's home and spent the next fifteen minutes trying to find the front door. When I did, no one was home. She had written the wrong time on her calendar, and energy was missing her. A main entrance on the side of the house is bad enough, but one on the back of a house is *least* desirable. If someone has to pass by one or more auxiliary doors on the way to the main door, it invites confusion in your life.

To avoid confusion, misunderstanding or lost opportunities, make it extremely obvious how to get to your front door. A spacious paved pathway to a hidden door is essential. Stepping-stones are not enough. Have motion, sound, and/or bright color near the door—all these attract attention, and that's your goal. Some suggestions: wind chimes, wind catchers or a fountain. If you have a hidden front door, refer to page 12, "Obscure Entrances," in *Feng Shui for Hawai'i.*

Stairs

There should only be one set of stairs leading to the front door. Two matching sets may look graceful, but they greet chi energy with a question mark: "Which way should I go?" It doesn't make a difference, but a

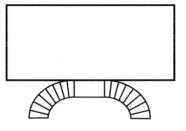

Do not have two sets of stairs at the front door.

person has to make a decision, and that very slight confusion represents dampening the enthusiasm coming to the door. The path should be clear, with no need for a guest to try to decide which way to go.

If your front door is directly at the top of a long flight of **yard stairs** (stairs that are just in the yard, not house stairs which are connected to the house or lānai) and faces those stairs, it symbolizes good fortune bouncing down those stairs

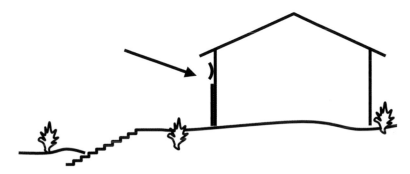

Yard stairs leading down in front of the front door signifies good fortune rolling away. Add a concave mirror to pull the energy to the house.

Yard stairs heading straight down to the front door signify energy hitting the door too harshly. Build up the threshold slightly.

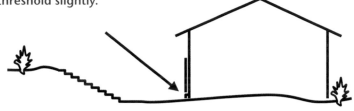

and leaving your house. Put a concave mirror outside the house just above the door. Because it caves in, it represents pulling the good fortune back in. State your intent—returning the good fortune—as you put the mirror up.

Then there's the opposite situation—your front door is at the base of a straight line of outside stairs. (With indoor stairs, the situation is not a problem.) Only a flight of many stairs—6 or more—creates a problem. The best solution is to raise the threshold of the front door. That is seen to block harsh energy, but don't let it block your feet—keep it low enough that it's not a tripping hazard.

Be it small or large, the lānai that's directly in front of the front door should not be semicircle-shaped. Think of the mouth of a measuring cup, where the pouring is done. That semicircular spout on the lip is for pouring liquids *out*. Any kind of semicircular landing at the base of the front

Top left: A semicircular shape outside the front door symbolizes good fortune pouring away.

Bottom left: This front lānai is tiny but very welcoming and shaped correctly.

Right: The shape of the doormat is a problem, but the door color is so powerful that it overcomes the situation.

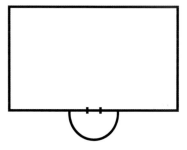

door represents money pouring out. It's best not to use a semicircular front doormat, for the same reason. Semicircular windows above or beside a door are not a problem, and can help balance the hard angles of the door.

Front Door Facing a Tree

It's especially important that a tree (or pole) is not in a direct line with your front door—between your door and the road. If the tree is off to the side, it's fine. It must be in an absolute direct line for it to be a problem. A front door opening toward woodland doesn't have this problem. There are trees in the woods, but they have a very different energy than a single solitary tree in the yard in front of the front door. There's a rare occurrence where a support post is directly in front of the front door. It's usually when the entrance is at a corner, and the door wall is at an angle.

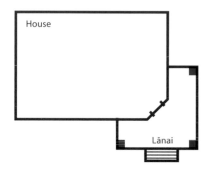

House

Lānai

A support post directly in front of the front door is a rare, but possible, occurrence. The blue posts here do not present a problem; however, the red post is directly in front of the door and symbolizes an obstacle.

There are two solutions if you have a tree or pole in line with the door—pick one or the other, but don't do both.

• A bagua mirror placed outside, above the door, is best. Aim the mirror toward the base or the lower trunk of the tree. A Seal of Solomon mirror will also work. *See Glossary for more information on these mirrors.*

• You can also change the purpose of the problem tree or pole. Instead of being an obstacle, you can turn it into a holder-of-affirmations by placing a written affirmation in the tree or on the pole. The affirmation can be as small as one word, such as "Love" or "Peace." If the tree has a low, wide crotch, you could place a stone (with affirmative words carved into it) there. If the tree branches are higher, don't use anything heavy—perhaps, instead, use an affirmative coin such as those used by recovery groups. You can also etch your own affirmation by softly impressing words onto metallic food wrap foil. A good example: "Look up, be well." A single word is equally as effective. Press lightly with something like a dull pencil. The affirmation can be hidden in the tree (or on the post)—it doesn't have to be seen to work. You put it there; it's working for you.

There's one situation in which a tree in front of a front door is perfectly fine—when a road is aimed at the front door. In this instance, the tree breaks the impact of the harsh chi. A large tree is perfect because it can also break the impact of a vehicle before it hits your door. *See Chapter 3, "T-Intersection," pages 79-80.*

Water

Water represents wealth in feng shui, and the similarity in the Hawaiian language is quite noticeable—"wai" means fresh water; "waiwai" is wealth. The connection between prosperity and money is why fountains are an important feng shui tool. Fountains are always good near a front door *if* the flow of water is toward the home. Fountains that flow in all directions are also good, because some of the water

A working fountain near the front door represents prosperity flowing. Just be sure that at least some of the water is flowing *toward* your home.

Still water near the front door is also excellent, as long as the water is not stagnant.

moves toward the home. Water is also a neutralizing agent, so harmful energy is nullified before affecting the home.

Still water, such as a birdbath, is also excellent near the front door as long as the water stays clean. *See also: Chapter 2, "Bird," pages 57-59, and Chapter 4, "Pools and Ponds," pages 108-112.*

BRINGING BALANCE

A feng shui garden brings a feeling of balance to the property around your house. The balance of the landscape signifies better balance in your life and within the home. The garden also provides a very basic feeling of protection. That feeling of protection is at the root of feng shui. The old feng shui masters studied the action of nature on various sites. Does this cliff crumble away? Do floods occur here? Do tsunamis affect this shoreline? These places don't convey long-term stability. Places that are a bit tucked away—ones that feel physically supported and out of danger—are judged to be more stable in feng shui.

The Armchair Position

The ideal sites have a surrounding landform represented by these four animals: black Turtle (behind), red Bird or Phoenix (in front), green Dragon (masculine, and to the right, as you stand outside facing the building), and white Tiger (feminine, and to the left). These are very protective energies that support a home in the way a good armchair supports someone sitting in it. That's why this landform arrangement is commonly referred to as the armchair position, also sometimes called the horseshoe.

The land behind the home, represented by the Turtle, should rise up and away from the house, but not too steeply. The land in front of the home, represented by the red Bird, should slope down and away from the home, again not too steeply. If there is a natural water feature, it should be in front of the home site, not behind it. Each side of the home should have rises that are fairly equal in height and form; however, the dragon side should be a bit taller. These two rises should be lower than the rise behind the home—think of the armrests of a chair.

Here's the ideal: the rise behind the home is the highest; imagine that as one full unit. On the right (Dragon, masculine) side of the home, the height is 3/5 of that unit, and the land on left (Tiger, feminine) side of the home is 2/5 of that unit. (Males are statistically a little taller than females.) The Bird can be indicated by a small rise of earth or plants in the front, but nothing that interferes with the open view.

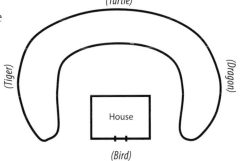

(Turtle)

(Tiger)

(Dragon)

House

(Bird)

A good armchair position is fairly easy to create with hedges in a horseshoe shape around the home. The hedges substitute for the hillside. Refer to the lists of hedge plants on pages 64-69.

A house in the armchair position is powerful because the land protects it without obstructing it. The down-sloping land in front gives people in the home an awareness of what is approaching. Homes with this landform

Opposite: Just like a person in an armchair, the home should sit comfortably in the landscape.

The armchair position supports the home. Homes with this landform configuration are so strong, any other feng shui problems are made less serious.

configuration are so strong that any other feng shui problems are made less serious.

Dragon

If the rise on the Tiger side is higher than the Dragon side, or if the Dragon side slopes down, you need to strengthen the Dragon side.

Ideally, cars should be parked on the Dragon side because cars are powerful and strengthen the protective energy of the Dragon. If cars are parked on the Tiger side, the Tiger energy can become stronger than the Dragon, and that's not the right balance; the Dragon should be the most protective energy. If cars are parked on the Tiger side, strengthen the Dragon side.

The easiest way to strengthen the Dragon side is by installing a dragon sculpture. It doesn't have to be fancy and expensive—cement is fine. You could also put any item with a dragon image outside on the right side of the home. The item could be a glazed pot, a bell or a banner.

If you use garden sculpture to represent any of the four animals, the statue should face the same direction the home's front door faces, or toward the entry of the property. The sculpture thus greets the arriving energy.

The Dragon is represented by the color green (so nearly any plant would work), but when strengthening the Dragon energy it's good to also use red. Red is the color of the Phoenix in the front yard, but it's also the most yang color since it's the color of fire. Fire is considered to be the most yang (active), and water is the most yin (passive) element.

Left: This colorful dragon figurine is appropriate for a shaded lānai, but it would fade if placed in direct sunlight.

Middle: This pot shows a dragon protecting the nyoi jewel, the gem of enlightenment. The plant in the pot is dracaena, which means "dragon."

Right: A dragon bell is good to strengthen the Dragon side of the home.

The "fire" of electric lighting (including solar) is a good Dragon strengthener, as is an outside grill, especially if it's used frequently.

The botanical name for the dragon tree means "dragon dragon." It's obviously related to the money tree, but seen less often.

Plants with an upward form and plants that climb upward are good on the Dragon side. Red bougainvillea is a perfect plant for the Dragon side, especially if you are able to let the branches get rather long. If you've got large bougainvillea beside your home, you will probably feel quite protected on that side!

There are plants with "dragon" in the name, such as the dragon tree, which are extremely appropriate to plant on the Dragon side. The dragon tree is closely related to the common money tree; its botanical name is *Dracaena draco*—both words mean "dragon," the first in Greek, the second in Latin.

POWER YOUR DRAGON

YOU CAN ALSO STRENGTHEN THE DRAGON SIDE BY CREATING HEIGHT AND MOVEMENT THERE. ONE WAY TO CREATE MOVEMENT IS BY ADDING A CLOTHESLINE ON THE DRAGON SIDE. THE ACTIVITY OF THE CLOTHES FLAPPING IN THE BREEZE IS YANG AND GIVES STRENGTH TO THE DRAGON. IF THE POLES RISE ABOVE YOUR HEAD, THAT CREATES EVEN MORE HEIGHT. BE SURE THAT CLOTHESLINES WITH HOLLOW METAL PIPES DON'T CREATE A RIFLE BARREL LINE

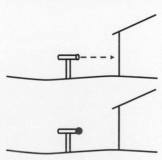

TOWARD YOUR HOME (LEFT, TOP). IF THERE IS A CLOTHESLINE IN THIS CONFIGURATION, SEAL BOTH ENDS OF THE TOP HORIZONTAL PIPES. THAT WAY YOU'LL COMPLETELY STOP THE GUN BARREL FEELING. IF YOU WANT IT TO BE EVEN FRIENDLIER, MAKE THOSE ENDS ROUNDED (LEFT, BOTTOM).

The metal supports of this clothesline aim up and away from the home.

Plant List: Plants with Dragon Names

· **Dragon Flower** (*Huernia* spp.)—a lanky, thorny cactus with deep red flowers.

· **Dragon Fruit** (*Hylocereus* spp.)—available with red or yellow fruit.

· **Dragon Tree** (*Dracaena draco*)—photo on page 51.

· **Dragon's-Eye** (*Dimocarpus longan*)—another name for the edible fruit longan, which is related to lychee.

· **Dragonwing Begonia**—a very carefree plant. It's usually found with green leaves, but there is also a kind with leaves that are almost all red.

Tiger

If the land slopes down on the Tiger side (the left side as you are facing the front door), plant upward plants. If they have white leaves or flowers, they are especially strengthening on this side. It can also strengthen this side to have a tiger sculpture—especially if the land slopes steeply down and away from the house here. Make very sure that the figure is a tiger and no other feline.

Turtle

The Turtle is a land turtle, not a honu (sea turtle), and it is represented by vertical lines. This is one of the reasons that a tree or pole in front of the front door causes problems, as mentioned in Chapter 1: the vertical line represents the Turtle and therefore should be in the back yard, but instead it's in a direct line with the front door—totally the wrong place. A vertical line also clashes with the open feeling that you want at an entry.

In feng shui, the landform (or built environment that substitutes for landform) around the house is either "protected and backed" or "exposed and vulnerable." A building is vulnerable if the land behind or on either side of it severely slopes down. If a house lacks protection on one or more sides—that is, if the land slopes down beside or behind the house—plant trees (preferably not deciduous) or tall shrubs on those sloped sides. Tall vertical trees are especially

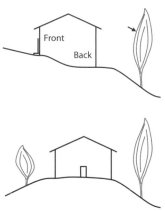

appropriate behind the house. In this position they truly feel like guardians and provide the correct upward feel.

Homes that are in very exposed locations (hilltops, ridge tops or right next to the ocean or a gulch) are usually located for the view. They are often expensive homes, but not always happy ones. That open exposure chips away at the house physically (with high winds) and also in a more subtle way that is important in feng shui. Planting protective vegetation that might block some of the view is rarely appealing to the homeowner. Palm trees can be a good compromise. Tall, non-clumping palms won't obscure a view and can make the view more romantic by framing it. Palms aren't as protective as denser trees, but tall palms with thick trunks do feel strong and mighty. Also, you can set out vertical plants that stay nice and low and keep an open view.

Left: The land slopes down in this back yard, but the far boundary has a tall panax hedge which supports the home.

Top right: If the land slopes down in the back yard, the home lacks support. Plant trees to symbolize support.

Bottom right: If the land slopes down on either side of the home, plant trees or tall shrubs.

GOOD VIBRATIONS

THE VARIEGATED SANSEVIERIA, *SANSEVIERIA TRIFASCATA 'LAURENTII,'* HAS A PARTICULARLY AGGRESSIVE UPWARD VIBRATION BECAUSE THE ANGLE IS REPEATED—ONCE IN GREEN, AND ONCE IN YELLOW. IF YOU PLANT FROM A LEAF CUTTING, THIS KIND WILL REVERT BACK TO THE PLAIN, NON-VARIEGATED COLORATION. TO KEEP THE VARIEGATION, THE CUTTING MUST HAVE SOME ROOT WITH IT.

Plant List: Upward-Shaped Plants

Low Upward Plants:

• **Parakeet Heliconia** (*Heliconia psittacorum* 'Parakeet')—the most common heliconia. Everything about it says, "Upward!" 📷 *A*

• **Parlor Palm** (*Chamaedorea elegans*)—the best small palm for a somewhat shady location. The botanical species name means "elegant," and it certainly is. 📷 *B*

• *Sansevieria trifascata*—see sidebar for photo

• **Succulents**—this class of plants includes many upward-growing options. Chandelier plant (*Bryophyllum (Kalanchoe) tubiflora;* 📷 *C*) has a decidedly upward form and never gets very tall.

• **Vanda Orchid** (*Vanda* spp.)—some orchids hang down and some go up. Vandas go up. 📷 *D*

A   *B*   *C*   *D*

Medium-Height Upward Plants:

• **Dracaena** (*Dracaena* spp.)—'Janet Craig' is a lovely plant with somewhat small, rich green leaves that give it a royal kāhili look. 📷 *E*

• **Pencil Tree** (*Euphorbia tirucalli*)—be careful how you use this unique plant; it can seem barren (even though it's not). It doesn't have much in the way of leaves; its fat green stems provide chlorophyll. It also has a caustic white sap for which euphorbias, in general, are famous.

Medium-Height Upward Plants:

- **Panax** (*Polyscias guilfoylei*)—the easiest and quickest upward plant. It grows from a stick cutting and does not become weedy or invasive. If it gets too tall, whack it back; it won't mind. There are quite a few different panax. 📷 *F*

- **Ti** (*Cordyline terminalis*)

- **Vetiver Grass** (*Vetiveria zizanioides*)—clumping and non-seeding, it is related to lemongrass, and its roots are used in the finest perfumes. It holds the soil against heavy rains better than man-made structures such as cement covering a hillside along a roadcut. Vetiver is ideal to plant along the top rim of a gulch—it's lovely and holds the soil. *See Resources, page 195.*

E

F

Tall Upward Trees

- **Bamboo**—available in many different heights, bamboo has a very pleasing upward form. The type pictured is the very interesting Buddha belly (*Bambusa ventricosa*). 📷 *G*

- **Italian Cypress** (*Cupressus sempervirens*)—the most common tall upward tree in Hawai'i, its shape is unmistakable as an upward symbol. They add exactly the right feng shui support, but people rarely want to use them where they would do the most good because the trees would obstruct a view. 📷 *H*

- **Norfolk Island Pine** (*Araucaria heterophylla*) and **Cook Pine** (*Araucaria columnaris*); both sometimes called columnar pine—tall and upward, they can look harsh and dominating in Hawai'i's landscape. Plant them with restraint. A cute little Christmas tree can become overpowering in little more than a decade here. If either of these two trees (which are sometimes mislabeled when they are sold) starts growing at a strange angle, take the tree out—it will never look right. If you can't bring yourself to cut the tree, plant a strong vine like liliko'i to obscure it. 📷 *I*

- **Palm**—usually quite upward, unless they lean from the tradewinds. Coconut palms (📷 *J1*) can make a stunning view even more tropical and romantic. Here their upward form provides support between the house and the ocean. The sealing wax palm (*Cyrtostachys renda*) (📷 *J2*) does double duty as an upward plant: its shape is vertical, and the red along the crown shaft symbolizes fire going up.

G   H   I   J1   J2

Shape is more powerful than color in feng shui. Imagine sitting on a lānai just after sunset, when you can no longer make out the color of an object, but the form or shape is still evident. An upward, vertical shape is the first choice to correct poor landform. But if form doesn't appeal to you (maybe it interferes with a nice view), you can always use color. The plant colors that lift energy the most are white and yellow—because they are bright like the sun. Red also lifts energy well because it represents fire, and flames rise upward.

Bird

The Bird is sometimes called the Phoenix, and is best represented by openness and a low hump, like a sprawling shrub. A plant could serve to represent a red bird. The slipper flower (*Pedilanthus tithymaloides*) looks like a red bird, and is sometimes even called the redbird.

Top: Pagodas are a graceful way to lift the energy of an area. Their shape is obviously upward, yet their heaviness gives them a balanced and grounded feeling.

Bottom: Slipper flower is also called redbird cactus. Growing in front of your home, it can represent the Red Bird.

MOA

I'VE READ THAT MOA IS THE OLDEST UNCHANGED PLANT ON EARTH. IT'S NATIVE AND COMMON IN HAWAI'I. "MOA" MEANS "CHICKEN" IN HAWAIIAN, SO IT IS VERY FITTING TO SYMBOLIZE THE RED BIRD THAT PROTECTS THE FRONT OF THE HOUSE IN FENG SHUI. YOU CAN GROW MOA ANYWHERE IN YOUR YARD, BUT IT'S ESPECIALLY APPROPRIATE IN THE FRONT. IT CAN GROW IN SUN OR SHADE, ON ROCK WALLS, OR IN TREE BARK. SOMETIMES IT JUST SHOWS UP BECAUSE OF SPORE DISTRIBUTION IN THE WIND, AND IT ALWAYS SEEMS LIKE A BLESSING.

According to feng shui, the front of the house is the ideal place for the best view, because the land should slope down and away from the home. This is how I advise clients who haven't yet built, and it can be quite tricky to do this when your property is on the makai side of the road. The critical thing to avoid: noticing a less important door before seeing the actual front door.

Strongly vertical forms are not appropriate in the front of the house. That includes most, but not all, palm trees. Occasionally there are homes with a wooden privacy screen built at the edge of the front lānai, directly in front of the front door. And sometimes the screens consist of separate vertical boards. If that's the case, use a climbing plant to tone down the verticalness. Growing the plant in a pot will keep it from becoming too vigorous.

I feng shui'd for a woman on the Big Island who had Japanese columnar junipers in a sparse row in her graveled front yard. I told her they reminded me of jail bars. She appreciated my frankness, saying that it rang true. She used to be quite mobile, driving herself everywhere, but now her friends and relatives had to drive her places. She decided to give her brother the columnar juniper and replace it with creeping juniper. The creeping juniper will also cover more of the gravel and give the yard a greener look, but still in the Asian style that she wants.

A stream in front of the home can symbolize good fortune coming in, and a stream or gulch behind a home indicates that good fortune is leaving. Water features such as ponds or fountains are perfect in the front yard; just make sure any direction of flow is toward the house. If the flow is away from the house and you can't change it, put any size mirror at the edge of the pond showing the flow reflected back toward the house. If a fountain flows in all directions, it is fine to use because *some* of the water flows toward your house. If, when a fountain is turned off, the water vanishes and the fountain looks dry—that's a bad thing. You're sending a message opposite to your intention. An empty fountain says, "Things are dried up around here." The best fountains, from a feng shui perspective, have a visible pool of water even when the motor is turned off.

Water symbolizes abundance, and when it's outside the front door, it's ready to come right in. ✍

Hey, Good Lookin'

Because the Tiger and the Dragon are female and male, respectively, it's possible to place appropriate images outside to attract a person of a specific gender into your life. If you're looking for a woman, put a feminine image on the left side of the front door or yard—perhaps a sculpture. If you're looking for a man, do the opposite: put a masculine image on the right side of the front door, or on the right side of the yard—it doesn't have to be directly beside the door. I don't recommend using religious imagery for this purpose, because the religious figures represented were usually celibate. Once you've got your partner, the figure should be removed. Be grateful for what you've got, express your appreciation and don't keep looking.

A masculine image, such as this Green Man, can be used to attract a man to the house. Place it outside the front door to the right of the door. A female figure should be placed on the left side to attract a woman.

OFFERING PROTECTION

Using your garden to protect your home is an extremely powerful way to strengthen your life. Use plants or other objects to undo the influence from harsh or negative energy, known as sha chi or shar chi in Chinese. It's not an energy that can be measured, but it symbolizes a harshness or foreboding quality in an object or structure. Windows and doors are more vulnerable parts of the home structure— they are where an intruder would enter—so be sure to protect those areas especially well.

Let's examine the solutions first; then we'll consider why you might need them around the house.

Solutions

When there is a disturbing influence in the environment that cannot be removed or changed, there are three kinds of feng shui solutions:

- Block it or screen it so you don't see it.
- Reflect it back with a mirror or reflective ornament.
- Disperse it with an object such as a cut crystal.

You can use one or more solutions. The first one is the best because the disturbance is physically blocked off and cannot be seen from the house—out of sight, out of mind. Then the yard can be a peaceful buffer zone surrounding your home. The extra peace is real, and it is felt by the residents and all who enter.

The last two kinds of solutions are purely symbolic. You are doing little to the physical environment yet hope for a great reduction in harsh energy reaching the home. Add emphasis, focus and power with your voice—say what your intention is when placing symbolic solutions. Your intention can be whispered or said loudly, whatever is appropriate in the circumstance. You don't have to repeat your intention or even think about it again, but do keep the object (crystal or mirror) clean.

Block It

Visually erasing a problem view or object is as close as you can get to *actually* erasing it. Enclosing your property with a solid wall or hedge is sometimes the secret to creating a more peaceful yard and home. The wall can be stone, wood, plastic or even fabric. Walls are often the best option for a small yard. The wall or hedge should be at least ten feet from the house, to allow room for peaceful energies to accumulate on your side of the wall. You don't want a cramped feeling between your home and the surrounding wall.

Hedges and trellises are the loveliest way to block harsh energy. Plant an evergreen hedge that, as much as possible, can't be seen through. If you're in a windy and rainy area, don't use plants that have very flexible stems, such as Mexican flowing bamboo. It's best to plant all of a hedge at once. If you leave gaps to plant in later, those plants will be

Opposite: Blocking an immovable or undesirable object from sight with a wall or screen is the best way to combat a problem view.

greatly disadvantaged because of root and light competition from the established plants, and the result will not be what you hoped for. There are many possibilities for beautiful hedge plants in Hawai'i.

PLANTING PANAX

HERE'S WHAT NOT TO DO WHEN PLANTING PANAX—DON'T PUT THE STICKS IN AT AN ANGLE. THE PLANT WILL NEVER CORRECT THAT ANGLE AND WILL ALWAYS LOOK STRANGE AND DISTURBING.

Plant List: Hedges

- **Dracaena** (*Dracaena fragrans*)—often called corn plant, but it's not edible and its only fragrance is at night. If you want a hedge that thrives in the shade, don't bother reading the rest of this list—dracaena is the plant to pick. If watered properly, it will keep its lower leaves for many decades, even in very gloomy shade. Corn plant is also available with white or yellow-stripe variegation on the leaves, which can certainly brighten up a gloomy location. *Dracaena hookeriana* (📷 *A1*) has extra-large leaves. 📷 *A2*

- **Areca Palm** (*Dypsis lutescens*)—an areca hedge looks absolutely tropical. You won't see this in a temperate zone. 📷 *B*

- **Bamboo** (*Bambusa multiplex* or Malay Dwarf)—don't plant just any old bamboo and expect it to be a good hedge. Chose well and you won't be sorry—there are quite a few different cultivars within the multiplex species alone. A multiplex bamboo hedge looks fine whether trimmed or left natural. These plants can even grow well in (heavy) lānai containers because they are very tight bunching and accept pruning well. Be sure to plant only clumping bamboo in Hawai'i. Running bamboo can turn into a monster, and your neighbors would soon hate you. Usually, the best place to buy bamboo is from a nursery that specializes in bamboo. 📷 *C*

Plant List: Hedges

- **Beefsteak Plant** (*Acalypha godseffiana*)
- **Be-Still** (*Thevetia peruviana*) and **Oleander** (*Nerium oleander*)—work as hedge plants, although I can't recommend them because they are so poisonous.
- **Blue Vitex** (*Vites trifolia*)—known as lagunding dagat in the Philippines.
- **Bougainvillea** (*Bougainvillea* spp.)—makes a hedge that is as good as a wall for keeping people out. 📷 *D*
- **Brazilian Red Cloak** (*Megaskepasma erythrochlamys*)—looks rather plain until it blooms, but then it's quite extraordinary. It flowers in Hawai'i during summer and fall. It looks best untrimmed. 📷 *E1, E2*
- **Chinese Hat Plant** (*Holmskioldia sanguinea*)—also called cup-and-saucers, although it's a different species from the cup-and-saucers on this list. It can be pruned or left unpruned.
- **Coral Aphelandra** (*Aphelandra sinclairiana*)—the brilliant flowers impart a gracious tropical look, but it's best suited to wet, windward locations. It won't look its best as a formal trimmed hedge.
- **Crepe Myrtle** (*Lagerstroemia indica*)—available with purple, pink or white flowers.
- **Croton** (*Codiaeum variegatum*)—makes for a thick hedge with tropical exuberance. 📷 *F*
- **Duranta** (*Duranta erecta*)—also known as golden dewdrop, it grows well even in dry locations. There are several varieties available. 📷 *G*
- **Fishtail Palm** (*Caryota mitis*)—for a tall, thick hedge, fishtail palm is perfect. The clustering fishtail palm continuously sends up new stems to replace the old—that's important because these palms die after flowering and fruiting. 📷 *H*
- **Gardenia** (*Gardenia augusta*)—one of many fragrant plants that can be used as hedges. 📷 *I*
- **Hibiscus** (*Hibiscus* spp.)
- **Juniper** (*Juniperus* spp.)—Juniper makes a very neat trimmed hedge. Across the road is an areca hedge. 📷 *J*
- **Lavender Cup-and-Saucers** (*Holmskioldia tettensis*)—should be kept cut back when used as a hedge.
- **Mirror Plant** (*Coprosma repens*)—can be pruned or left in its natural form. The variegated mirror plant has very shiny leaves. 📷 *K*

continued on next page

Plant List: Hedges
continued

- **Mock Orange** (*Murraya paniculata*)—the most pruneable of hedge plants, if you like a manicured look, but it also looks fine unpruned, as a more low-maintenance option. In full sun it makes a dense hedge. 📷 *L*

- **Natal Plum** (*Carissa macrocarpa*)—the flowers are fragrant, the fruit is edible and the thorns are serious—Natal plum is quite a hedge plant. 📷 *M*

- **Panax** (*Polyscias guilfoylei*)—some folks say this plant encourages termites, but the truth is, any plant encourages termites if not pruned correctly. Always prune branches at an angle, not flat on top. If the top of an upward branch is cut flat, it rots before it can heal the wound. Then termites or ants make a home in the soft rotten material. The variety pictured has a bit of white variegation around the edge. 📷 *N*

- **Plumbago** (*Plumbago auriculata*)—has joyful blue flowers in addition to being a excellent hedge. 📷 *O*

- *Podocarpis chinensis*—called maki in Japanese. It has very graceful leaves and is usually kept pruned. It can reach 60 feet, so it's not good in every circumstance. For shorter plants use kusa-maki or inu-maki (*P. macrophyllus*). 📷 *P*

- **Poinsettia** (*Euphorbia pulcherrima*)

- *Pseuderanthemum carruthersii*—looks like croton, but it's not. It can reach 10 feet high, and there are three leaf colors commonly found in Hawai'i: purple, yellow and variegated. 📷 *Q*

- **Rhapis Palm** (*Rhapis excelsa*)—my favorite for sunny (or partially shady) situations. When it gets thick, it creates a totally opaque screen. It's elegant, but expensive. 📷 *R*

- **Snowbush** or **Laukalakoa** (*Breynia disticha*)—the standard variety (📷 *S1*) is commonly used, but be aware that its roots are invasive. It can grow to 10 feet tall. Dwarf snowbush (📷 *S2*) grows slowly and is not invasive, but it's often best for a low hedge—where definition, not a visual barrier, is wanted. The botanical name is the same for the regular snowbush and the dwarf, so be very sure you are getting the type you want.

- **Sugar Cane** (*Saccharum officinarum*)—can eventually make a fine hedge, in the right situation. It's especially lovely if you remove lower leaves to reveal the stems—some Hawaiian varieties have very colorful stems.

- **Ti** (*Cordyline terminalis*)—to really work as a hedge it must be planted very thickly.

A1

A2

B

C

D

E1

E2

F

G

H

I

J

K

L

M

N

O

P

Q

R

S1

S2

Plant List: Native Hedges

- **A'ali'i** (*Dodonaea viscose*)—accepts clipping well.
- **'Ākia** (*Wilkstroemia uva-ursi*)—use the upright kind for hedges.
- **Alahe'e** (*Psydrax odorata*)—accepts clipping well and will work as a windbreak.
- **'Āweoweo** (*Chenopodium oahuense*)
- **Hau** (*Hibiscus tiliaceus*)—the variegated type doesn't get as large as the regular. Holds up well to trimming. 📷 *A*
- **Hibiscus** (*Hibiscus* spp.)—the native hibiscus, koki'o 'ula'ula, makes a very effective hedge, trimmed or untrimmed. The native white species, *Hibiscus arnottianus* and *H. waimeae,* are often preferred over the red, because they are not susceptible to blister mites. The white blossoms are fragrant, too. 📷 *B*
- **'Ilima** (*Sida fallax*)—good as a low hedge, since it only grows to about four feet tall. It can become weedy, however. 📷 *C*
- **Kolomona** (*Senna gaudichaudii*)
- **Kokia** (*Kokia* spp.)—accepts clipping well.
- **Ko'oko'olau** (*Bidens menziesii*)
- **Kou** (*Cordia subcordata*)
- **Kulu'ī** (*Nototrichium sandwicense*)
- **Maiapilo** (*Capparis sandwichiana*)
- **Milo** (*Thespesia populnea*)—good when you need a large hedge, but it can be clipped to keep it under control. It has beautiful heart-shaped leaves and can grow right down to the ocean's edge. 📷 *D*
- **Naupaka Kahakai** (*Scaevola taccada*)
- **Noni** (*Morinda citrifolia*)

A

B

C

D

A wall that is also a trellis is excellent in feng shui for protection, privacy and peace.

Plant List: Trellis Plants

A

- **Allamanda** (*Allamanda cathartica*)—beware of how vigorous it can be. The flowers are graceful and available in a variety of colors. 📷 *A*

B

- **Angel-Wing Jasmine** (*Jasminum laurifolium*)—a charming plant, it has a sweet scent that is not overpowering. It's not as fragrant as some other jasmines, such as pīkake. 📷 *B*

- **Bleeding Heart** (*Clerodendrum myricoides*)—can be grown in the ground or in a pot on a lānai. The Hawaiian name is hō'ehapu'uwai. 📷 *C*

C

- **Carolina Jasmine** or **Yellow Jasmine** (*Gelsemium sempervirens*)—the flowers smell nice, but all parts of the plant are poisonous if ingested, so do not plant it where children will be playing.

- **Clerodendrum Vine** (*Clerodendrum ×speciosum*)—the purple and red flowers are quite a delight, but it is a more delicate vine. It will not tolerate harsh winds or dry weather. 📷 *D*

D

- **Coral Vine** or **Chain-of-Love** (*Antigonon leptopus*)—as tough as it is beautiful; it will tolerate wind and dry weather. The flowers are pink and very eye-catching. 📷 *E*

- **Gloriosa Lily** (*Gloriosa superba*)

E

- **Gourds**, including **Ipu** (*Lagenaria siceraria*) and **Luffa** (*Luffa acutangula*)—these are not perennial plants, so replanting is required.

- **Hoya** (especially *Hoya carnosa*)—nicely fragrant, a bit like baked bread. The drops of nectar on the flowers are edible and delicious.

F

- **Kūhiō Vine** (*Ipomoea horsfalliae*)—pink is the color of love in feng shui, and it's easy to love the pinkish-red flowers of this vine. 📷 *F*

Plant List: Trellis Plants

G

- **Liliko'i** (*Passiflora edulis*)—looks good, smells good and tastes good. It grows quickly and covers a trellis thoroughly. 📷 *G*

- **Mandevilla** (*Mandevilla* ×*amoena*)—'Alice du Pont' is the most common pink variety. The flowers are romantic and showy. 📷 *H*

H

- **Orange Trumpet Vine** (*Pyrostegia venusta*)—an easy way to bring brilliant color into a dry landscape. It's also called flame flower, or haupala in Hawaiian. 📷 *I*

- **Pakalana** (*Telosma cordata*)—its sweet fragrance is loved by all, and a trellis keeps the blossoms closer to nose level. There is also a large pakalana with the same fragrance.

I

- **Philodendron** (*Philodendron* spp.)—many to chose from, including the lovely type with velvet leaves. The juvenile leaves (pictured) are quite velvety; the adult leaves are bigger and longer and lack most of the fuzzy texture. 📷 *J*

- **Pothos** (*Epipremnum pinnatum*) or **Golden Pothos** (*E. aureum*)

J

- **Stephanotis** (*Stephanotis floribunda*)—another well-loved fragrant flower. Like most plants, it requires full sun to bloom in profusion. 📷 *K*

- **Tecomanthe** (*Tecomanthe dendrophila*)—has a delightfully exotic habit of flowering directly from its thick stem. 📷 *L*

- **Thunbergia** (*Thunbergia* spp.)—*T. grandiflora* has white flowers. *T. laurifolia* (📷 *M1*) has lavender flowers and is sometimes called laurel-leaved thunbergia, but it's also available with white flowers. *T. mysorensis* (📷 *M2*) has unique yellow and reddish-brown flowers. It's quite spectacular, but like many spectacular vines, it's a grower as well as a show-er. Be prepared to prune it.

K

L

M1

M2

Reflect It Back

Mirrors have three main uses in feng shui—to enlarge a space (*see page 99*); to draw energy into a space (*see Chapter 1, "Near the Door," page 41, bottom illustration*), and to reflect energy back, the main use. For reflecting energy back, there are three kinds of mirrors; they do three different things. Flat mirrors send energy directly back. Convex mirrors diffuse energy and send it in many directions. These are especially recommended to reflect back traffic and are readily available at auto supply stores. Concave mirrors absorb energy and reduce it. Concave mirrors are sold for make-up and shaving. To be properly effective, a mirror should remain clean, so check it occasionally and give it a wipe when necessary.

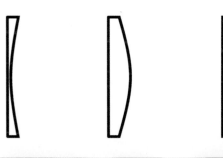

Top left: *Concave*—Absorbs and reduces energy.

Top middle: *Convex*—Reflects energy from many sources.

Top right: *Flat*—Pushes energy directly back toward the source.

Bottom: You can buy these small mirrors at your local craft store.

• When using a mirror outside the home, be sure it faces the problem directly. The mirror works best when it actually reflects *back* the image or images of the source of the problem. If there is a high hedge or wall and you can't see the problem from your house, try to put the mirror on the *outside* of the wall or hedge. If you can still see the problem from your window, use a mirror to reflect it back. It's not overdoing it to put a mirror above or below every window that faces the problem. A multi-story dwelling on a property with a fence or wall around the perimeter needs a mirror on each upper level of the building. I usually use dime-size mirrors from a craft store and stick them on with glue or double-sided foam tape.

• Ornamental silver glass balls can be used outdoors instead of mirrors. They look like garden decorations, which they are, but they also happen to do the feng shui job of reflecting back.

• Any shiny metallic object can be aimed at the harsh energy to reflect it back. In Hong Kong, the backs of shiny woks are sometimes hung outside to reflect away the harsh energy of a neighboring structure. A very shiny doorknocker is perfect if harsh energy is aimed at the front door.

Any shiny reflective object can be used to symbolize reflecting harsh energy away from your house. The object must stay well-polished to remain effective.

For severe problems, a **bagua mirror** or Seal of Solomon mirror is best. They both represent perfect order and balance. The Seal of Solomon is a symmetrical six-pointed star and is used in Hindu mandalas that depict balanced energy. (*See Glossary, page 192, and Resources, page 194.*) Any time I suggest a bagua mirror, a Seal of Solomon mirror will also work.

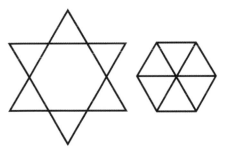

The Seal of Solomon (left) represents perfect balance. If all the triangles were folded in (right), they would perfectly fill the center space.

Don't put a bagua mirror any old place as a good luck charm, particularly above a door, to attract good fortune. That's not what it's for. The mirror part signifies reflecting away, and the trigrams around the frame symbolize perfect balance. An eight-sided mirror, without the trigrams, is not a bagua mirror—it's just an ordinary octagonal mirror. Plain round mirrors above a front door are often recommended by some consultants to attract energy because they are flashy and draw attention. I can only recommend that if it appeals to your sense of style—you don't want to repel your own aesthetic energy.

Protective mirrors outside your home are usually best placed above windows and doors, because those places are the most vulnerable parts of a home. A thief or intruder would enter through them, rather than break a new hole in the wall. If small flat mirrors are used, be sure to aim them exactly at the problem. Double-sided foam tape, cut into tiny pieces, works well to tilt them.

Disperse It

These are all symbolic solutions, so say out loud, at the time you install the solution, what your intention is: to disperse energy.

The occasional ringing of well-tuned wind chimes is very peaceful. Inharmonious or excessive sound can be nerve-wracking.

• Wind chimes or wind harps (sometimes called Aeolian harps) make the invisible energy of the wind audible, dispersing the energy of the wind into sound waves. Be sensitive when using wind chimes outside— ask other household members as well as neighbors if the sound disturbs them. The sound should be musical; I advise against clanking shells or tinkling glass pieces.

• Flags, banners, or wind socks flapping in the wind *is* the dispersing of energy. The movement of the fabric is the invisible energy of the wind, made visible.

• Pinwheels symbolically deflect and disperse harsh energy before it reaches your home. Although this is a "technically correct" solution, I'd be loath to do it unless you can find an attractive presentation using durable materials. Ordinary pinwheels will deteriorate badly outdoors and are often *so* brightly colored they're more gaudy than attractive.

• Clear crystals (natural or artificial) scatter the energy
of the sun into rainbows, so they are very commonly used in
feng shui to symbolize dispersing energy. If harsh energy is
aimed toward a window, it's good to hang a faceted crystal in
that window (inside the home) to symbolically disperse the
harshness. In many homes this is the only option. You can
use a disco-ball-shaped crystal or—for even more rainbows
inside your home—an octagonal crystal. Make sure the
crystal won't bump against the window if it gets breezy. You
may need to use a bracket to extend the crystal further from
the window glass. A little rubbing alcohol on a rag is the
simplest way to keep the crystal clean. If the harsh energy is
not visible from the window because of exterior screening
(such as hedges), the crystal is not needed in the window.

Problems

It's nice to have few worries. When I started learning feng shui I thought, "This gives a person a lot more to worry about than they already had to worry about." I laughingly refer to feng shui as "the art of paranoia." But the truth is, it's best to be akamai (knowledgeable) about what is "aimed" at your home or property. In a subtle way, when something is aimed at your home it chips away at the energy of the home, like a steel chisel chipping into stone.

Straight lines can be a problem in feng shui, especially when they are long enough to have a "rifle barrel" kind of energy. This caution is traditionally embedded into aspects of Chinese design. The straight lines of the then-new railroads and telegraph lines are part of what caused the Chinese Boxer Rebellion in 1900. The rural villagers were quite aggravated when these "improvements" came charging into their lives. Railroads and telegraph lines are *very* long and *very* straight. For centuries the villagers had carefully guarded against having too many straight lines, even building zigzag bridges wherever it was feasible. If a bridge was built in a straight line, a large stone would be placed at the village end of the bridge with an inscription carved into it, "This stone dares to resist."

Straight lines create fast, harsh energy, and that energy should not be aimed at your house. When a straight line (like a stick) bends and snaps, it can take the shape of an arrowhead. The energy that was racing along the straight line now races along two straight lines and zings off at the corner—just like an arrow. These right-angle corners are very common in neighborhoods. We'll look at them first.

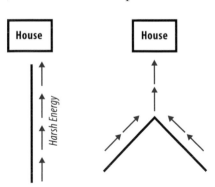

Opposite: A dead stump is an inauspicious view. Transform it with living energy in the form of new growth, either rooted directly to the stump, like this laua'e fern, or in an attractive planter placed on top.

Harsh energy can be delivered by a straight line or by an angle of two straight lines.

Poison Arrows

Poison arrows are also called "secret arrows," and they aim sharply and specifically. They usually come from the sharp corner of a neighboring structure. Imagine a sharp pencil held very close to—but not touching—your eye. Some people would develop a twitch even though nothing actually comes into contact with their eye. That's how poison arrows work. Divide a sharp right angle in half and extend the line to see where the corner aims. Use online satellite maps to see exactly where the corners of neighboring houses aim.

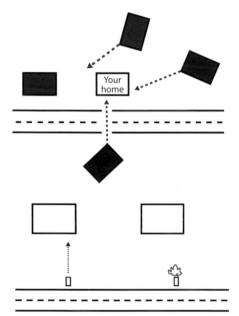

There are no poison arrows from the nearby structures in blue. However, poison arrows are directed to your home by the structures in red.

A mailbox by the road can create a poison arrow. You can block it by planting a thick shrub between the mailbox and the house.

If something doesn't aim at you, there is no need for concern. If an angle is larger than a right angle (obtuse) it does not create a poison arrow. If a neighboring structure is completely above or below the level of your home, the sharp side corners of the other structure do not affect your home.

Objects like clotheslines (*see Chapter 2, "Dragon," pages 50-52*), outbuildings (*see Chapter 4, "Structures," pages 103-105*) and even mailboxes can create poison arrows in your own yard. It's best if the rear of a standard freestanding mailbox doesn't "point" directly at the house. If it does, plant a shrub between it and the house.

The Road

Roads are rivers of energy with the potential to disturb a peaceful home. There are several circumstances where the energy of a road is not good for the energy of the house, and the basic structure of the garden can make a huge difference. It mostly depends on whether or not car lights can shine on your house. The car lights are the eyes of large, dangerous, metal beasts. If the lights can shine on your house it's bad enough, but if they shine into your windows, your peaceful home is truly being invaded.

Convex Side of Curved Road

The most common instance of headlights shining on a home is when the home is on the convex side of a curved road. That's the side of the road that bulges out. Think of a convex curve as the beginning of an angle pointing at you. It's like the blade of a curved knife, such as a machete, where the convex side is sharp and can do harm. The lights from street traffic are a very unwanted intrusion—they should not shine into your home's windows or onto the outside walls of your home.

Unwanted energy easily enters a home on the convex side of a curved road. The houses on the inside of the curve are protected.

Houses on the convex side should have an evergreen hedge or solid wall in front to protect them. If that isn't immediately possible, attach a convex mirror outside the front of the house. Try to place it at the height at which car lights strike the house. Because it bulges outward, the mirror reflects energy from many directions. Such mirrors are inexpensive and readily available where auto supplies are sold.

T-Intersection

When a building is at the exact end of a T-intersection it has harsh energy aimed at it. This is because the straight line of the road is like a gun barrel aimed at the house, with cars as the bullets. Sometimes cars even go out of control and hit houses in T-intersections. In feng shui a solid wall is best, and the higher the better. If you cannot add a wall, plant the most solid hedge you can afford. Never have your driveway in direct line with a T-intersection; harsh energy will rush down the road

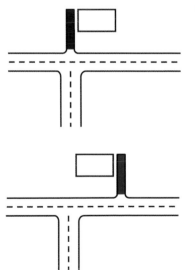

Left: Too much harsh energy enters this driveway (in red).

Below left: The best solution is to move the driveway (in blue).

onto your property. In this circumstance, it is best to move the driveway, or install a solid gate. If a T-intersection aims directly at the front door of the house, this is an instance when it's acceptable to have a big tree in front of the front door, just not too close. The tree absorbs the harsh energy, just as it would absorb the impact of a big vehicle.

In a cul-de-sac these three houses (red) are in problematic locations.

Cul-de-sac

Homes at the very end of a cul-de-sac are in a problematic location, as are houses that appear to be at the "neck" of a cul-de-sac. A house at the end of the cul-de-sac has a road aimed directly at it, so follow the advice for T-intersections. Houses at the neck of the cul-de-sac can have a problematic choking, or squeezing, energy due to their location at the point where the road changes from a straight road to a wider circle.

Roads that end in a straight line and have no cul-de-sac are not very fortunate in feng shui. Straight roads should have a circle at the end so cars can turn around gracefully. Houses that are very near the end of a road without a cul-de-sac are impacted by the stagnant energy that can accumulate at a dead end. If that's your situation, a bagua mirror outside over your front door will discourage confused energy from entering your home. If you live on a street that has a Dead End sign, don't refer to it when giving directions. There's better wording for those signs, such as No Outlet.

Busy Highway

A home right next to a *very* busy road, such as a freeway, suffers from having its energy chipped away. Each vehicle wears away at the vibrations of the home. Good, deep rest can be elusive for those living there. A thick hedge will help, but not as much as a tall stone wall. Also, add a convex mirror outside facing the road. A bagua mirror is quite appropriate in this situation.

Foreboding Objects

Foreboding objects are a large category in feng shui. Anything that looms over the home in a threatening way is doing the home and its occupants no good. People who are too close to the pali (cliff) usually have a feeling of being a little too close to the edge. Protruding boulders upslope from the home are also extremely unfortunate in feng shui. Besides natural landforms, the category of foreboding objects includes:

• The ocean—if it's right next door. A tsunami (or two) is quite likely to happen in Hawai'i in your lifetime. The best advice is to move further inland, but that advice is not likely to be heeded. At a minimum, plant palm trees between your home and the ocean.

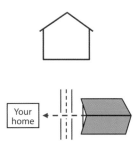

This roof shape should not face your house.

• The sharp angle of a rooftop should not be directly across from your house. However, consultants differ in opinion here—some say the arrow of the roof points upward and is harmless.

• A very tall building that is out-of-scale for the neighborhood, and extremely close to your home, is too big and should have a concave bagua mirror aimed at it.

• Construction sites are a harsh influence upon a quiet home, even if the work is being done on your own property.

• Low airplane flight path. If it's possible to move, do so. Otherwise put a bagua mirror on the roof.

• A vacant, littered lot. Pick up the trash, and the chi will change dramatically.

Screening trash cans from constant view helps the chi energy of a home enormously.

• Trash cans on your property don't have a foreboding energy, but they symbolize

uselessness and should be screened from frequent view.
A fragrant vine on a sturdy metal fence is ideal. Be sure all
trash cans have covers that fit well.

• Police or fire stations. The bells and sirens and sense of
emergency are too harsh to be close to a home.

• Mortuaries have too much dead energy. Belief holds
that a confused spirit can linger in the close proximity of
its iwi (the remains of its old physical body) for up to forty-
nine days.

• Cemeteries—for the same reason as above.

• Hospitals—same as above. Also, the sound of the
ambulance siren is too harsh to be close to a home.

Even churches are not considered appropriate neighbors
when they are directly next door to a residence and if
funerals are held there. This is because of the possibility
of wandering, confused spirits—in feng shui that is taken
very seriously. Also, many churches sit vacant and unused
for long periods of time and therefore take on a very yin
vibration, which should not be right next to regular homes.
It's certainly okay for ministers and priests to live near their
churches. An excessively sharp steeple—as some churches
have—has a threatening, sword-like physical presence. If the
church doesn't have a sharp steeple, isn't used for funerals
and is in active use most days of the week, there is no
problem with living next to it.

Schools are not problem neighbors in feng shui because
of the young, active (yang) energy there. Thankfully, this
hasn't been much of a problem in Hawai'i, but schools with
a history of gun violence can become not-so-good feng shui
neighbors. Keep all schools safe places—it creates positive
energy for the children and for the neighbors.

A view of a dead tree fairly close to your home does not
bode well. That's especially the case if it's the first thing
you see as you leave your driveway, or the first thing you
see when you get home. Some feng shui consultants advise

removing the tree, but
that's not always possible
or desirable. Plant a vine
or vine-like plant to
quickly cover and add life
to the dead tree. Several
scorpion orchids, planted
at the base of the dead
tree, would look quite
exotic—they can quickly
obscure a tree. *See also:
Chapter 4, "Maintenance,"
page 151.*

A dead stump is not
an auspicious view in
your own yard, even
if you're the only one
who sees the stump. A
stump with chainsaw grooves cut into the top has generally
had poison applied to it; the grooves allow the poison to
penetrate into the plant. That kind of stump may not rot
easily, depending on the kind of poison that was used.
(The microorganisms that cause rot don't do well with
some poisons.)

When I need to remove a stump, I cover it with black
gardening plastic to encourage it to decompose. Hide the
black plastic with paper or mulch so it doesn't degrade
in the sunlight, and to make it more attractive. Plant
something that will quickly obscure the stump; a creeping
plant such as hearts-and-flowers would be excellent, or
put a big potted plant on it. Once the stump is dead and
beginning to decay, remove the plastic so the earth can
breathe again, but leave the plantings that obscure the
stump until it completely rots away.

A big metal drain grate in front of your house is a source
of foreboding energy. A small curbside cement drain is
discreet and of much less concern. If you must drive or step
across a metal drain grate in or near your driveway, you need
a tiny mirror—half-inch diameter or less. Glue it under the
bottom of the metal grate with the shiny side aimed down

Top left: Vibrant
colors and living
plants overcome the
dead energy of this
tall stump.

Top right: Staghorn
fern has certainly
changed the dead
feeling of this tall
palm stump. To move
a staghorn keiki
(called a pup), tie it
to the new location
with nylon stockings
and cut the stocking
away when the pup
has adhered to the
tree surface.

Bottom: Hearts-and-
flowers can easily
cover a low stump.

to reflect away the energy of the drain. The best glue I've found for this is Mach 5, which is sold in beauty supply stores for gluing acrylic nails.

Be very aware of the views from your windows, one of the most important aspects of the garden. The window views set a tone for our interaction with the world. The kinds of plants that are close to the house (and especially their leaf shape) should be given great attention. I had a client, in one of the drier parts of Kona, with two grammar-school-age children. The children each had separate bedrooms, and the parents wanted to plant huge agave outside their bedroom windows. The mother was concerned that as the children grew older, they would slip out of the house at night. I told her that although the agave would grow well there, it had too threatening a shape for directly outside a child's window.

Top: Plants that look as stiff and sharp as agave should not be the predominate view from any window or lānai.

Bottom: If you need a thorny plant near the house for security reasons, use one with hidden thorns such as Natal plum.

I suggested Natal plum instead. It has fragrant flowers, edible fruit and horrible thorns, but the thorns are well hidden beneath round leaves. It has a friendly look but will still discourage physical contact. I find *Feng Shui & Your Health* to have the most detail about plant views from windows. *See Recommended Reading, page 187.*

Very unfriendly neighbors are another type of foreboding energy. "A slight boost in neighborly trust has a greater effect on happiness than doubling your income," says Christopher Barrington-Leigh, co-author of a University of British Columbia study. To help

create peace and harmony, put plants that you love along
the property line of unfriendly neighbors, especially if the
plants have fragrant flowers. You are installing sweetness
and love between you and the problem people. The best
colors to plant between unfriendly neighbors are pink or
yellow. Avoid red because it can signify fiery energy. If you
feel the need for a thorny plant as a hedge on that side
of your property, I recommend Natal plum because it's
fragrant, or pink bougainvillea for the color's association
with love. When you look in their direction, your concern
should not extend beyond your property line; take joy in
your beautiful plantings and do not let the negativity on
the other side intrude.

There is a category of foreboding objects that the ancient
Chinese feng shui masters didn't have to be concerned about:
electromagnetic fields (EMFs)—magnetism generated by
electricity. This energy can be measured with a gaussmeter.
The high electromagnetic field around electric substations can
extend more than one block. Don't live closer than two blocks
from an electric substation. *See also: Chapter 4, "Electromagnetic
Fields," pages 156-157.*

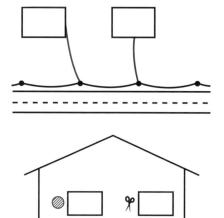

An electric power pole
with a transformer on it is
a foreboding object, even
if strong EMFs don't reach
your home from it. The
harsh industrial look of the
transformer is considered
threatening. The electric
line, telephone line and
cable line are all straight
lines. Unless they are
buried, it is important to
notice how they meet the
home. It's best if electric
lines come to the side of the
house so they do not form a straight line aiming at the home.
If electric lines mar a lovely view (even just a view of the
sky), you can place a mirror facing the lines, or hang a pair of
metal scissors outside the window or door that faces the lines.

Top: Be aware of how
electrical lines meet
your home. The line
marked with blue is
not a problem, but
the one in red aims
directly at the house.

Bottom: If a window
or door faces electric
lines, hang a mirror
or metal scissors
facing the lines.

The scissors symbolize cutting the lines out of your view; they should be metal—a stronger substance—rather than plastic. And, of course, I trust you have better sense than to try to actually cut or move an electric line that spoils your view.

If an electric power pole has a cross piece, its shape isn't good for your home. An electric power pole that has staggered metal bars up the sides for climbing is called a centipede pole

Top: An electric pole with metal spikes for climbing is called a centipede pole and is inauspicious.

Bottom: Chickens eat centipedes. Keep a live chicken or a rooster figurine or image between your home and a centipede pole.

because the bars look a lot like legs. That kind of pole needs a rooster aimed at it. Chickens eat centipedes, and roosters are the fiercest chickens. The rooster figurine can be any material that will look appropriate outdoors. Use only one—no cock fights. You could also put a rooster figurine inside a window, facing the pole. If you have a chicken coop, you can put it between the house and the pole. As with any outbuilding, don't let the coop make a poison arrow toward the house.

The rooster figurine solution is not recommended for people who were born in a Rabbit year— Rabbits and Roosters are not compatible in the Chinese zodiac. In this case, or if chickens do not appeal to your sense of style, use a crystal or mirror instead.

This last topic is a controversial one—jagged mountains. The everyday view of jagged mountains is viewed by some feng shui consultants as inauspicious. That's because the jagged shape on the horizon is perceived as unpeaceful, no matter how beautiful. The windward view of the Ko'olau Mountains is widely acknowledged as one of the most beautiful views in Polynesia—and the beauty is not just in the lushness, it's the dramatic shape as well. I used to live on that side and I love it. Seeing that view feeds

From a feng shui standpoint, there's more to the beautiful Ko'olau Mountains than meets the eye.

a person's spirit—how could it not? Well, the one little picky feng shui thing is: it's not inviting. Something that is eroding so quickly (relatively speaking, in geologic time) is not stable to climb on and wander around. You must take extreme care when you're on the ridge top. That sense that "you must be cautious if you're here" is all it takes for some feng shui experts to have a problem with it. I wouldn't dream of covering the view—from a yard or from a window. If you're concerned about it, or are experiencing problems, hang an octagon crystal in any window of the house that faces toward a view of jagged mountains.

Now for the other point of view: if the jagged mountains are lush—extremely so—that makes them a living Dragon, and a living dragon is a very positive influence. Mountains (and hills), which represent Dragons in feng shui, are classified as either living or dead Dragons; the big difference is *life*. If there's abundant life in the landform, the Dragon is alive.

GARDEN MISCELLANY

There are many considerations involved in creating and maintaining a garden with good feng shui. The locations of buildings and features in your garden have an impact on the feng shui of the space. Choose and place items mindfully. Problems and opportunities, large and small, can arise when dealing with the great outdoors. Work with nature and your own creativity to create a peaceful and balanced environment around your home.

Property Shape

Square-shaped properties are perfect, and rectangular lots are also good if the width and length are somewhat similar. Rectangular properties that are long and skinny (spaghetti lots) are problematic in feng shui. People generally sense that the energy doesn't coordinate well from front to back on the lot. In this instance, don't let the back of the property became stagnant and unvisited. Create inviting trails leading to the very back of the property.

Trapezoidal lots are fairly common, and there's no universal agreement about their meaning. Some consultants feel the largest side should be at the front to invite energy in, like a funnel—but others say the largest side should be at the back to catch the "wealth energy" that accumulates there.

If a corner of your property forms an acute angle, the energy there is being squeezed; make that area feel more expansive. Lighting will do that, even little solar lights. Another way to expand an acute angle is to use plants with white flowers or leaves with white variegation.

Most flowers are white, in general, and particularly, most flowers with fragrance are white. Most of the choices on the list of fragrant plants in Chapter 5 can be used when a white flowering plant is called for—picking from that list will make this world a sweeter (smelling!) place. Listing all the white flower plants would be too massive an undertaking, but here are some that are easy to come by or produce masses of white.

Money Bag lot shape

Dust Pan lot shape

These two lots are both trapezoidal, but the Money Bag lot shape is good, while the Dust Pan lot shape is not.

White leaves are brighter than green leaves, so they are more yang and expansive. This symbolism of expansion is used to "enlarge" a tight property corner.

Opposite: Because the flowers of this vinca are bright they expand garden areas that feel tight. A white leaf or flower reflects chi energy from the sun into our eyes, creating the perception of brightness.

Plant List: White-Flowering Plants

- **Alyssum** (*Lobularia maritima*)

- **Anthurium** (*Anthurium* spp.)—an exotic-looking workhorse of a plant. Once they are established, a shady area is transformed. 📷 *A*

- **Hibiscus** (*Hibiscus* spp.)— koki'o ke'oke'o is the native white hibiscus of Hawai'i. Its beauty rivals the finest hybrids. 📷 *B*

- **Impatiens** (*Impatiens walleriana*)—white impatiens can make a dark area positively glow. 📷 *C*

- **Pentas** (*Pentas lanceolata*)—needs full sun to bloom well. 📷 *D*

- **Spathiphyllum** (*Spathiphyllum wallisii*)—also called peace lily.

- **White Bush** (*Euphorbia leucocephala*)—produces white bracts at the same time as poinsettia, and the two related plants look fabulous together. Other names for it are white lace and pascuita.

A

B

C

D

It's amazing how many green-leafed plants that easily spring to mind also have cultivars with white colorations. From monstera to rhapis palm, white makes a striking appearance in leaf color. This is far from an exhaustive list, but a good start.

Left: Occasionally, variegated monstera will produce a completely white leaf, which is quite a sight.

Right: Variegated rhapis is my favorite palm. It's as interesting as a bouquet, and it's quite easy to grow. The trick is finding one.

Plant List: White-Leafed Plants

- **A'e A'e Banana** (*Musa* spp.)—pronounced "ah-eh ah-eh." The magnificent leaves light up a tropical landscape, and even the peel of the delicious fruit is variegated. Other names for this maoli (native) plantain are koa'e and manini. It's a Hawaiian banana, and as such is susceptible to a root beetle that isn't much of a problem in other kinds of bananas. To outrun the beetles, you have to move all the keiki to new locations. Do this immediately following fruit harvest. If you let the keiki stay in the old location, the root beetle will find them. 📷 A

- **Blue Vitex** (*Vitex trifolia*)—the cultivar 'Variegata' has white in the leaves.

- **Caladium** (*Caladium bicolor*)—the leaves often have plenty of white. 📷 B

- **Costus** (*Costus speciosus*)—available with white variegation—the variety is 'Variegatus.' 📷 C

continued on next page

A   B   C

Plant List: White-Leafed Plants
continued

- **Dieffenbachia** (*Dieffenbachia* spp.)—can have the whitest leaves imaginable. 'Rudolph Roehrs' is quite bright.

- **Dwarf Bamboo**, Variegated (*Phyllostachys* spp.)—a groundcover. Like any bamboo, it can be very difficult to remove, so many gardeners prefer to plant it in a confined area. 📷 *D*

- **Dwarf Snowbush** (*Breynia disticha* 'Minima')— 📷 *E*

- **False Oregano** (*Plectranthus amboinicus*)—has fuzzy leaves and is a very vigorous groundcover, so plant with care. 'Variegata' (📷 *F1*) has white in the leaf. It smells a lot like true oregano (*Origanum vulgare;* 📷 *F2*), which makes a well-behaved groundcover (though it lacks any white coloration).

- ***Ficus benjamina***, Variegated 📷 *G*

- **Gold Dust Dracaena** (*Dracaena surculosa*)—very easy to grow and looks bright even in a shady environment. The variegation is usually more white than yellow. 📷 *H*

- **Hibiscus** (*Hibiscus* spp.)

- **Lucky Bamboo** (*Dracaena sanderiana*)—there are several kinds with white coloration in the leaves.

D E F1

F2 G H

Plant List: White-Leafed Plants

- **Pothos** (*Epipremnum aureum*)—the cultivar 'Marble Queen' is quite white.
- ***Sansevieria trifasciata* 'Bantel's Sensation'**—this variety has brilliant white stripes on the leaves.
- ***Sansevieria trifasciata* 'Moonglow'**—the new growth starts out powdery white but changes to green with age. 📷 *I*
- **Spider Plant** (*Chlorophytum comosum*)—well-known and can brighten a dark cliffside because the keiki hang down naturally. The 'Vittatum' variety has about 50% white leaves. 📷 *J*
- ***Stromanthe sanguinea* 'Tricolor'**—this lovely plant isn't as common as it should be. White seems to be the predominant color. It's incredibly exotic; the visual energy of this plant is quite yang. 📷 *K*
- **Swedish Ivy** (*Plectranthus verticillatus*)—available with white variegation, 'Variegated Mintleaf.' It can be weedy, like false oregano—they are closely related.
- ***Talinum fructicosum variegate***—the bright leaves are edible, like purslane.
- **Ti** (*Cordyline terminalis*)—some cultivars have quite a bit of white with almost no red, such as 'White Rain' and the even whiter 'White Rain Number 2.' 'Lovely Hula Hands' and 'Philippines' also have very white leaves.

continued on next page

I

J

K

Plant List: White-Leafed Plants
continued

- **Variegated 'Ape** (*Alocasia macrorrhizos* 'Variegata')—quite a showstopper, and it does well in shade. 📷 *L*

- **Variegated Ginger** or **'Awapuhi Kī'oki** (*Alpinia vittata*)

- **Variegated Hala** (*Pandanus tectorius*)—hala looks very tropical and romantic because of its droopy leaves. The variegated kinds are even more exotic, and bright variegation can be unexpected on a large plant like this. 📷 *M*

- **Variegated Lemon** (*Citrus limon* 'Pink Eureka')—both the fruit and leaves have variegation. The inside of the fruit is pink; pink lemonade is a bonus. 📷 *N*

- **Variegated Money Tree** (*Dracaena marginata*)—does a powerful job of lifting energy because of its brightness and upward form. 📷 *O*

- **Variegated Spearmint** (*Mentha ×spicata*)—doesn't require as much water as peppermint. The Hawaiian name is kepemineka. 📷 *P*

L

M

O

N

P

Just as with white-leafed plants, there are very many kinds of yellow-leafed plants. Almost any plant that has white in the leaves is readily available in a yellow-leafed variety as well. Yellow is used to uplift, but it can also scream. It's almost as attention-getting as red. Make sure you find the yellow in the leaf pleasing to your eye.

Plant List: Yellow-Leafed Plants

- **'Eldorado'** (*Graptophyllum pictum*)—similar to a croton, and this cultivar has very yellow leaves.

- **Golden Pothos** (*Epipremnum aureum*)

- **Golden Prince Aralia** (*Polyscias filicifolia* 'Golden Prince')

- **Pandanus** or **Hala** (*Pandanus tectorius*)—there are variegated varieties in both regular and dwarf sizes. The dwarf is *Pandanus baptistii*, sometimes called pygmy pandanus. 📷 *A*

- ***Sansevieria trifaciata*** 'Laurentii'

- ***Schefflera pueckleri***—the variegated variety is quite striking. I believe it was formerly named *Tupidanthus caluptrius*. 📷 *B*

- **Ti** (*Cordyline* spp.)

- **Variegated Cassava** or **Tapioca** (*Manihot esculenta* 'Variegata')

A

B

Plants with yellow flowers, like white-flowered plants, are too numerous to list. Yellow is a happy color, and it's the second most common flower color in nature. Here are just a few.

Plant List: Yellow-Flowering Plants

- **Allamanda** (*Allamanda cathartica*)— available in several colors, but yellow is the most common. That's why it's known as cup-of-gold.
- **Daylily** (*Hemerocallis* spp.)—here you have a huge selection of yellow shades. The Hawaiian name is līlia pala'ai. 📷 *A*
- **Galphemia** (*Galphemia gracilis*)—my favorite; there's one on each side of my front stairs. They never stop blooming throughout the year. 📷 *B*
- **Hibiscus** (*Hibiscus* spp.)—ma'o hau hele (📷 *C1*) is a bright and easy-to-grow native hibiscus. Other types can have lively red centers. 📷 *C2*
- **Pincushion Protea** (*Leucospermum* spp.)—at higher elevations, protea provides soft yellow flowers in a full-sun location. 📷 *D*
- **Yellow Kou** (*Cordia lutea*)—has yellow flowers for most of the year. 📷 *E1, E2*
- **Yellow Poppy** (*Eschscholzia californica*)—for brilliant yellow color in a dry landscape try poppies; this plant is very drought resistant. 📷 *F*

A *B* *C1* *C2*

D *E1* *E2* *F*

Mirrors can expand a space symbolically and are often used indoors for that purpose. A discreet way to use mirrors to expand a tight-angled corner on your property is to position the mirrors at the edge, near the corner, facing inward. Announce something like, "These mirrors are symbolically expanding this part of the property."

Triangular lots are the worst shape. It is very important in feng shui to have four corners, which, of course, triangular lots don't have. Something is definitely missing—some energy in the residents' lives will likely be more or less absent. Even less fortunate is a home where the front door faces the acute angle of a triangular lot. In this case, put a bagua mirror over the front door on the outside.

The best action to take in any instance of an unusually shaped lot is to use border and hedge plantings to define a square or rectangular yard around the house. Try to redefine the corners of the yard as close to right angles as you can get them, given your circumstances.

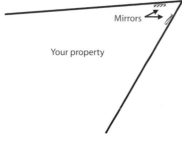

Mirrors

Your property

Place small mirrors to enlarge a tight corner.

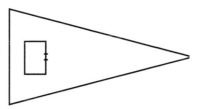

A front door facing a severe acute angle of your property says things are going to be squeezed.

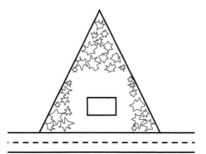

A square-shaped yard has been created on this triangular lot by filling in the angles with shrubs.

Location of House and 'Ohana on Property

Good fortune symbolically accumulates behind a house. The front yard invites it, and the back yard holds it. The back yard should be as big as, or a bit bigger than, the front yard. If the back yard is significantly smaller than the front, good fortune has a hard time accumulating. If the back yard is too small:

• Put a mirror at your back property line to symbolically expand the back yard. The mirror can be small, and it should face in, toward your property. If the back yard is tiny, and enclosed by a wood fence, consider putting a large mirror on the fence. It will really make the property seem larger. Unfortunately, mirrors don't fare well outside (in the weather) in Hawai'i—the silvering corrodes quickly. If you use large mirrors outside in places where they cannot be cleaned easily, it's often best to situate them behind plants, so you're not tempted to look at yourself. Seeing your darkened image in an aging mirror is not auspicious. Any large mirror that you can see yourself in should show your whole head.

• Add lighting (solar lighting is fine) in the back yard. The lights do not have to be turned on every night, but they do need to be kept functional.

• Paint a trompe-l'oeil mural on the back fence. "Tromp-l'oeil" is French for "fool the eye." Paint a scene with depth of perspective. This, too, will make the yard seem larger.

If there is a slope, the owner's house should be higher than the 'ohana (or rental) house.

If there is a separate unit on your property, occupied by family or renters, it should be in a less powerful position than the building occupied by the owner of the property. On sloping property, the owner's house should be higher than the 'ohana unit. On flat property it is best if the owner's house is further from the road than the 'ohana.

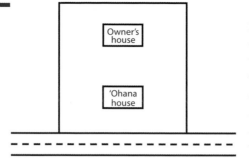

The owner's house should be farther from the road than the 'ohana house.

If the 'ohana is in the more powerful position on the property, put the owner's picture in the 'ohana unit. The occupants will need to be advised that the picture should not be moved. It will probably need to be in a discreet place, but be sure it is *not* in an area near drains. Also, plant a hedge to screen the view of the 'ohana, which is "lording over you."

Structures and Large Objects

Water catchment tanks are always round and therefore do not create poison arrows. They are fine in feng shui and an excellent way to mālama i ka 'āina— care for the land.

A single ti plant is not thick enough to block a poison arrow. Use a thicker shrub to block harsh energy.

Preceeding page: A hale has no walls and therefore does not create any poison arrows, and it can be located anywhere on your property.

Gazebos, outbuildings, hot tubs and the like should be round so they don't aim poison arrows at the home. Water catchment tanks are always nicely circular, and they must be located based on the roof drainage. They usually do not pose a feng shui problem, as they are stable and feel safe. Water is yin and is inappropriate to have beneath a yang dwelling. Rarely, but on occasion, the tank is inauspiciously located directly under the home and cannot be moved—what do you do? Use a mirror and/or crystal between the floor and the top of the catchment tank to reflect back and disperse that amount of water to keep it from affecting the home. Catchment and greywater collecting on the property are not problems from a feng shui point of view. They connect our land more closely with the energies of the atmosphere. Rain is the premier energy of the atmosphere.

A Polynesian hale (or bale) with no walls at all does not create poison arrows because there are no walls to conduct energy in straight lines. Hale can be anywhere. Homes with thatched walls do not create poison arrows because

the bound-up leaves don't make lines that are straight enough to speed energy along. Thatch is one of the most interesting kinds of walls—and that *interest* means that chi energy lingers; it doesn't just zoom along. But if an outside building has one or more standard walls, it needs to be located carefully, so as not to aim a poison arrow at the home. If a poison arrow is aimed at the home and you can't change it, plant a very thick, bushy shrub—

not something spindly like ti. Plant it as in the figure illustration to buffer the sharp energy. If possible, plant it closer to the poison arrow corner (the source of the problem) than to the house. Done correctly, planting can make a corner (and poison arrow) disappear.

Your home

The shrub location in red is not the best. It's best to place the shrub close to the poison arrow (blue).

A moon gate is a beautiful round opening in a wall. These gates originated in China and might look out of place on some properties. If a moon gate fits in well with your garden, and you have the notion to build one—do it. It will enhance and attract energy greatly, simply because it is so beautiful and unique. Moon gates call to us to walk through them, which means they invite energy to come through, too.

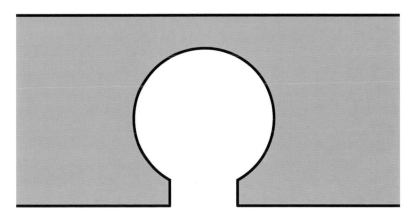

A moon gate is a lovely way of attracting positive energy.

Paths and Bridges

Paths and bridges should meander a little—not be laid out in long, straight lines. (A very short path can be straight and presents no problem.) Straight paths conduct energy too quickly and are too yang for home gardens. They can work in commercial landscapes where their function is different. Paths to and around your home should have a bit of a curve or meander. This is especially important for long paths and those leading to your front door. A path can also be too yin—too narrow and crowded. Tight, narrow paths pinch energy. That can be fine for a seldom-used trail in the woods, but the main pathways to your home need to be fairly clear and open for energy to find you easily.

It's quite unusual to find a garden bridge in Hawai'i that's long enough to classify as a poison arrow. But if the bridge is part of a long straight path, it's part of a poison arrow—and you can stop it by creating a meander with curves or zigzags, or perhaps irregularly-placed stepping stones.

Light pathways at night if you use them at night. There's no need to leave path lights (or any outside lights) on when they're not in use. The natural order is for the night to be dark, and feng shui is a natural art.

This homeowner has done several things to prevent energy from moving too quickly along this straight pathway. Energy is slowed by the use of separate pavers instead of one long strip of cement, and the small, rounded stones around the pavers feel yin and welcoming. Further to the right, the low stone wall creates a slow and gentle feeling because of its irregular lines and moss, which looks old and yin. On the left, interesting plants in gorgeous pots attract our energy and slow us down.

Opposite: The multiple fish and dragonflies in these stepping stones represent good relationship energy because the animals are not alone. Molded stones are preferred to those decorated with mosaics—which have the vibration of breakage, since broken pieces of pottery are used to make the image.

Pools and Ponds

The worst location for an in-ground pool is unfortunately where most are placed—directly behind the house. It symbolizes an abyss and fails to give the home proper backing and support. Any other location is preferable. However, if the pool is in the back yard:

• Place a small mirror outside the house facing the problem pool. The mirror pushes away the influence of the pool.

• I've seen planters that glow in the dark. They are perfect to put between the house and the pool. (*See Resources, Rotoluxe.*) Sansevieria is an excellent plant to grow in them, but anything with an upward form is good.

• In any planter between the house and the pool, add little glow-in-the-dark glass ornaments. They're attached to copper tubes that stick in the dirt and are available in many garden supply stores.

• Add upright plants, even potted plants, between the house and pool—the taller, the better. They lift up the area and create a separation. *See Plant List: Upward-Shaped Plants, pages 54-55.*

The pool should not be located higher on the property than the main house. Oval, kidney and free-form (in that order) are the favored feng shui shapes for pools. Round is fine too. If a pool is kidney or freeform shape, the concave part should be positioned closest to the house. The area

Left: This kidney-shaped pool does not embrace the house.

Right: This kidney-shaped pool embraces the house and is better.

Above: This kidney-shaped pool is oriented correctly; the convex edge of the pool is away from the home.

Right: Put potted plants between the pool and the house.

Pond water should look fresh, not stagnant. Moving water represents income, and the flow should be directed toward your house. Still water represents assets—money in the bank.

inside a curve is more protected than the outside (convex) part. Rectangular and square pools are not recommended. They are the most common shapes, though— so it's good that the solution is simple. Set a big round planter, with luxuriant plants in it, between the corner of the pool and the house. If the corner of the pool does not point at the house at all, there is no problem and no need for the planter.

An infinity-edge (sometimes called horizon, disappearing or vanishing-edge) pool is fine if the water flows only toward the house. If the water lip flows away from the home, that screams, "Lack of support. Money flowing away." For pools that flow away from the house, the best thing is to add some plants on the makai side to poke up over the edge of the pool. Sansevieria works well because it can handle full sun, pools usually being situated at in the sunniest part of the property, but it also does well in shade.

Small decorative ponds are best in front of the house. Any water flowing into a pond should be directed toward the house. If it's flowing away from the house, it's usually not feasible to change the pond, so place a small mirror on the side of the pond, slightly above water level. The mirror should

show the water flowing
back toward the house. Say
out loud what you intend to
accomplish with the mirror.

Water symbolizes
money in feng shui, and
moving water and still
water have different energy.
Still water represents
assets and moving water
represents income. The water should be fairly clean or
covered with plants, such as azolla fern (*Azolla filiculoides*),
water hyacinth (*Eidhhornia crassipes*) or water lettuce (*Pistia stratiotes*). It's fine to see the source of moving water, but
it's inauspicious to see the place where the water actually
leaves your property—assuming the moving water is a real
stream, which it sometimes is in Hawai'i. If there is natural
water (moving or still) at the edge of your property, it affects
you just as if it were completely on your property. Cultivate
sprawling plants to obscure the place where the water leaves
your property line. Naupaka is a good choice for many areas,
or go to any knowledgeable nursery and ask for sprawling
plants. They'll say, "That's easy—it's much of what we have."
Many of the plants that do well in temperate zones tend to
get very lanky in Hawai'i. Plus there's a seemingly endless
number of tropical plants that naturally sprawl, such as
firecracker, allamanda and thunbergia.

If you can stand next to your house and see water, either
in your own yard or in the distance, it's a good idea to put
a mirror on that outside wall. When you look toward the
house the view in the mirror will show the water, so it's as if
you are drawing that bounty into your home. Say out loud
that the mirror represents drawing prosperity in, or words to
that effect. In some instances, such as on a lānai, it can be
appropriate to use a very large mirror. That's a wonderful way
to get a beautiful ocean view twice. When it's not feasible or
attractive to use a large mirror, use a small one.

A Water Dragon refers to a type of dragon which can be
on the earth's surface, below the earth's surface, or in the
sky as clouds. Because it's reputed to increase good fortune,

Left: This fountain is
aimed away from the
home and represents
money flowing away.

Right: Instead of
turning the fountain
around, solve the
problem with a small
mirror facing the
water flow. The mirror
symbolically reflects
the water back toward
the home.

Source of
flowing water

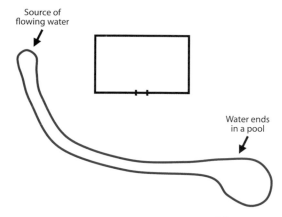

Water ends
in a pool

A basic Water Dragon.

people have tried for a long time to create an ideal (artificial) Water Dragon situation around their own dwelling, and they still attempt it today. According to the Landform School of feng shui, a Water Dragon is formed when the water source is located on the Tiger side of the house with a stream gently flowing to the Dragon side, past the front door. The water's path can go anywhere in the front yard, including near the front door, where it can create a memorable entrance to the home. Once the water moves to the Dragon side, it shouldn't appear to flow straight off your property. There should be a small pond where the water ends to signify that the good fortune remains on your property. Lillian Too's *Practical Feng Shui Formulas for Success* has detailed directions for creating Compass School Water Dragons according to the direction of the front door.

Don't create a dry streambed-look in your garden with gravel—it looks barren and lifeless. Instead, use creeping, prostrate plants instead such as juniper. You can even add a bridge over them if they are very low. A dried-up pond or fountain in your yard is bad feng shui. An ironic example can be found in front of the Board of Water Supply in Honolulu on Beretania Street. Keep fountains in good working order. Underwater lighting is not recommended. *See "Lighting," next section.*

Left: A dry streambed symbolizes that things are dried up. In this case, the energy of the red color of the bridge symbolically fixes the situation.

Right: Prostrate juniper turns a barren area into an area full of lush chi energy.

Lighting

The most natural gardens are dark at night, relying on moonlight for illumination. If artificial lighting is added, keep it mostly along pathways for safety. Try to disturb the natural yin darkness of night as little as possible. Even if you have lighting installed, use it only when necessary; there's no need to turn on the lights all the time. Light also attracts night-swarming termites—and you don't want *their* chi energy. The number-one rule regarding exterior lighting: *Don't create strange shadows.* If anyone living in the house is uncomfortable with the pattern of the shadows, try to adjust the lighting location or plant material. It is especially important that the head(s) of the household be very comfortable with the shadow patterns. One of my favorite shadow patterns is that of palm fronds, especially in a gentle breeze.

Lights can be added to create safe walkways, but there's no need to turn them on all the time.

I'm not a big fan of glow-in-the-dark objects—I think they're kind of spooky. The one exception is when a pool is in a back yard; any kind of light is good between a pool and a house.

The most natural outdoor lights are candles and torches—they add atmosphere as well as illumination. Exterior candles need hurricane shades around them in windy areas.

Solar lights are eco-friendly, and many styles and shapes are available. If there are pathways that are used at night, illuminate them gently. Strands of tiny clear (white) lights are enchanting, but don't use strands of multicolored lights outside except during holidays. If you use fixtures with right-angle corners, be sure that they don't aim a poison arrow at any

Candlelight is very natural outside, and a hurricane shade protects the candle from breezes. Also, this octagonal tabletop does not create poison arrows; the corner angles are greater than ninety degrees.

nearby seating area. Round fixtures are better.

Solar lights generally use LED bulbs that flicker—a feng shui problem; the flickering symbolizes instability. The quality of light is always more peaceful with a bulb that doesn't flicker. Some people notice the flicker of a light bulb more than others. Many people are "used to it," but on a subtle level they're still being affected by it. The light from LED bulbs does not mix well with other lights, so they are best used where people do not congregate—such as on stairs and pathways. Although they are small, LED bulbs can emit a piercingly strong light. To create a gentler glow, you can tape a small rectangle of waxed paper into a cylinder and use it as a shade around the bulb.

Fluorescent bulbs also flicker, including compact fluorescents, which are a sadly misguided effort to save money now at the expense of future generations. Fluorescent bulbs of any kind always have mercury in them, and the government asks us to dispose of them as **toxic waste**. Failure to do so means mercury enters our precious water table and, eventually, the coral reef system.

Incandescent bulbs should be used in outside areas where people gather. If you use bulbs with strong filaments they'll last longer, which is a big plus in some hard-to-reach outside fixtures. Incandescent bulbs are growing more energy-efficient and they don't flicker—unless the bulb is designed to imitate candlelight. That type of incandescent flicker is perfectly fine and can be charming outside. You can purchase incandescent flicker bulbs that use just two watts and will last indefinitely.

This large-filament bulb imitates a candle flame nicely, especially under a lampshade. It uses only three watts of electricity. The bulb is shown with a small chandelier base, but it also available with a standard base.

GLARE

NEEDLESS TO SAY, DON'T POSITION LIGHT BULBS (ESPECIALLY CLEAR BULBS) SO THEY SHINE DIRECTLY INTO SOMEONE'S EYES WHEN THEY ARE SEATED. ALSO AVOID SHINING LIGHTS AT WINDOWS. RATHER, AIM THE LIGHT TO SHINE ON A WALL. CAPIZ SHELL SHADES ARE PERFECT FOR OUTDOOR LIGHTS. THEY'RE NATURAL, THEY CREATE A SOFT LIGHT AND IT'S RARE TO FIND A CAPIZ SHELL SHADE THAT'S NOT WELL-ROUNDED. CLIP-ON CAPIZ SHELL LAMPSHADES ARE SECURE IN THE WIND. USE LOW-WATTAGE BULBS (I SUGGEST 15-WATT) TO TRULY SHOW THEM IN THEIR BEST LIGHT.

There are several instances when exterior lighting solves feng shui problems. Spotlights or pole lights are frequently recommended, but any light—even a tiki torch or outside candle—is better than none. (Never place live flames very close to a wooden building. Not only is it a real, physical danger, but to do so would invite stress to your life, even if only subconsciously.) The light does not have to be used every night to be effective, but it must be in good working order. Once a month is fine for turning on a light meant to fix a feng shui problem. You certainly don't have to leave the light on all night—a minute or so is ample. Here are examples of the use of exterior lighting in feng shui:

• If the backyard slopes down and away from the house, aim a light at the house. Its energy supports the house—lifting it with its light. (Take care not to aim the light at any windows.)

• If a corner of the property comes to a sharp acute angle, add a lighting element. In this case, the light is not aimed at the house, but illuminates the property in that area, symbolically enlarging it.

• If a cliff rises very close to the back of the house, aim a light at the cliff. The light symbolically pushes the cliff away.

Absolutely do not place lights below water. If such lights are already installed on your property, I recommend you don't turn them on. The feng shui symbolism is obvious in nature: fire under water—conflict. Instances of fire under water in nature are rare—you might see it in Puna on the Big Island of Hawai'i when lava flows out through a tube under the ocean. It's a dangerous, chaotic, explosive environment.

Lights shining *on* water are lovely and present no feng shui problems. Made Wijaya, author of *Tropical Garden Design*, says, "Lighting the inside of water bodies should be avoided. It just highlights muddiness, or, in swimming pools, simulates a nuclear reactor effect. It is best to leave water bodies dark, to reflect light." He also says, "Coloured lights can cause emotional distress in seniors." Pools should be a watery color such as blue. Never paint or tile your pool a fiery color, such as red. It's fine to have light shining down on water, but don't float candles on water (the fire is too close to the water).

Furniture

y favorite outdoor seats are Chinese glazed pottery garden stools. They're fun to sit on, they look great and are easy to clean, and they can also be used as tables or stands. They don't tend to blow over, so I always recommend them for O'ahu high-rise units with balconies. They're even fun to shop for because there are so many kinds and colors. They're not great to relax on, but you can use them as tables while lounging on something softer.

Seating that moves is a pleasant addition outdoors. There's a soothing joy that comes from gently rocking. The seating could be a swing or hanging chair, or a glider that sits on the ground. On a lānai with a smooth floor, like wood or cement, a rocking chair (or two) is wonderful. Don't place rocking chairs on tiled floors—it's not good for the chair or the floor.

Seating is often placed so that it draws the eye—that's yang (public) seating. The view of the seating beckons your whole body, and before you know it, you find yourself wandering over. If the yard is spacious enough, try to include seating in a hidden

Chinese garden stools are always interesting and delightful. They are lovely in the yard or on a lānai. They're also wonderfully multi-purpose.

Left: A swing that hangs safely from a strong natural tree limb is preferred to an artificially supported swing. But any swing at all is better than no swing. Children benefit greatly from swings, and they are good for adults too.

Bottom: A glider is a very comfortable and supportive way to enjoy a rocking motion while viewing your garden.

area to create an outdoor garden "room." This kind of environment is yin—more private and contemplative. This area doesn't need to have a roof over it unless that would encourage more frequent use. A garden room can be created with shrubs and vines— a simple setting of quietude, away from bustling activity. One or more sides of a garden room can be open to a view of nature. A more open space will have fewer mosquitoes.

Top right: A round table is always the best choice because it is the shape of heaven, but this table, with its rounded corners, also has good energy.

Don't place seating beneath hanging objects. If something dangles over your body, it is foreboding. I consulted for a nice ocean-side home where an exotic sculpture was hung outside above the front door, forcing anyone over five feet tall to stoop to enter the home—not good. Beware that a "unique effect" may create other problems.

Middle right: This dining set is carved from stone and makes a lovely landscape enhancement.

A round or octagonal dining table is preferable, both outside and within a home. In feng shui, a circle (an octagon is close to a circle) is the shape of Heaven, and a square is the shape of Earth. Heaven is more perfect than Earth; therefore, circles are more desirable shapes.

Bottom right: Generally, outdoor wooden tables should be sheltered during wet weather, so make sure they are lightweight and moveable. This lovely table is too heavy to be moved easily, but some weathering works well with its natural design.

There's another reason for using lānai furniture without sharp right angles. Just as the sharp right angle of a neighboring building can aim a poison arrow at a home, the sharp right angle of a lānai table can aim a poison arrow at someone sitting in a chair. A glass lānai table must have a covered rim; the bare glass edge has harmful "cutting energy."

These tables have no cutting energy because there are no bare glass edges.

Left: This table has a bare glass edge and therefore has severe cutting energy. Use a tablecloth over it until you can replace the table.

Right: Friendly, rounded edges, such as these tables and chairs have, are excellent.

Sculptures and Ornaments

Statuary in a natural setting seems more real and can create quite an attractive atmosphere. Just don't get carried away with ornaments and garden trinkets—more than a few can make a place look cluttered.

Some people *like* fu dog statues, while other people think they *need* fu dog statues to protect their home. The truth is, you can protect a home well without sculpture. If you have

fu dog statues and want to place them correctly, first you need to know—is this really a fu dog or is this a Chinese lion? They both have a protective influence on the home, and the dogs and lions can look very similar. Both types of statues properly come in pairs. Lions will have one of the pair (the male) resting his paw on a ball and the other (the female) placing her paw on a little cub. Put them flanking your front door. The male goes to the right of the door, as you face the door. The female goes to the left. The statues face forward to greet the energy that is arriving.

Fu dogs, on the other hand, belong in the backyard. Wealth symbolically accumulates in the back; the dogs protect it there. If you have real dogs, they can run anywhere on your property, but the actual doghouse should be in the back. People born in a Dragon Year should not have fu dogs because Dogs and Dragons are highly incompatible.

Statues of seated religious figures are best placed on something flat and stable that uplifts the figure in a respectful way. Religious statuary featuring standing figures can be upraised

Opposite: Written prayers, affirmations, and scripture verses are excellent in gardens, but should be used with moderation. One is usually plenty. Here, a poem is written beautifully on a large ceramic column.

Left: Chinese lion statues belong in the front yard. They look similar to fu dogs, so be sure you know what you have.

This Chinese immortal is nearly life-size. The figure includes a dragon and two children, so there is good relationship energy even though it is one statue.

Top left: This is Hotei. His name means "hempen bag" because he always carries a bag. He is often misidentified as "fat" or "laughing" Buddha, but those are incorrect names; he is actually a bodhisattva. There is no "fat" or "laughing" Buddha.

Top middle: This Ganesh statue is quite stable, but it would be better if it *looked* less precarious.

Top right: Standing religious statuary does not require a platform. Here, St. Francis looks very natural in a wedelia groundcover.

Top: Support platforms beneath seated statuary should be at least as big as the base of the statue.

Bottom: A platform below this seated statue would convey more respect and keep the grass from growing over it.

or on the ground. A stand, called a plinth, can be pohaku (stone) or cement. The top of the plinth should be larger than the bottom of the statue; otherwise a vibration of instability is introduced. If you want to burn incense or a candle in front of the statue, a flat, stable surface for the burning object(s) should be added. Outdoor incense burners are usually filled with coarse sand, and the incense is placed upright. The container must have a hole in the bottom for water drainage. If the incense burner has three legs, one of the legs should face directly forward toward you, representing putting your best foot forward. Incense burners used inside a building don't require holes in the bottom—they shouldn't ever need to drain. Indoors, a lightly-packed ash (instead of sand) is usually used to hold the incense upright. A full figure of a religious person is best, rather than just a head—it too closely resembles a severed head. It's good to have religious statues blessed by a priest or minister. Many cultures have this tradition.

If there are statues of people or animals in the front yard, they should appear to greet you as you arrive. Their back (or tail) should not face the entrance from the street—it's not welcoming.

Avoid populating your garden with statues of creatures (human or animal) that are all single and separate. One or two solo figures are fine, but with more the message can be, "There's no relating going on here." Either use statues that have relating built into them (more than one figure in the sculpture, *see photo, page 123*) or else group some single figures together. Grouping can be tricky because the figures should be

approximately the same scale—as if they could be having a conversation together. More than once, I've seen groupings that looked like big Buddha and little dog Buddha, because the proportions were quite different.

Driftwood is not appropriate inside a home because it symbolizes dead, stagnant energy. But outside, it's back in nature where it belongs and the negative symbolism no longer applies. Outdoors, its symbolism is strength and endurance. Some feng shui practitioners don't approve of seashells inside a home because they are technically dead. I don't take that hardcore approach, especially for exceptional shells, but large numbers of nondescript shells are best kept outside, if at all.

A Peace Pole is a four-sided pole with a beveled top. The phrase "May Peace Prevail on Earth" is written on each side in various languages. I've seen quite a few of these in Hawai'i, usually in the front yard so that people passing by can see them. However, because their vertical shape represents the Turtle, they are best placed behind the home. It would also be acceptable to place one on the Dragon side (the right side of the home).

When placing a sundial, the first priority is positioning it for full sun. The feng shui use is to attract chi energy,

Left: Sculptures in pairs or groups bring good relationship energy to the property. Locating the cranes near a water feature gives them more authenticity, and the round leaves of the water lily add a special gentleness.

Right: Any decorative ornamentation outside should look stable and balanced— not just balanced.

Put a sundial in a sunny area. A sundial looks silly in a shady location.

which happens simply because they're interesting. Almost no one uses them to regularly tell time, but they're fascinating to look at. If you have a path to a sundial, people will follow it—they almost can't help themselves. If there's a sunny part of your yard that you wish people (including yourself) visited more frequently, a sundial can be the draw. Even bright, open areas of a yard can grow stagnant if no one ever goes there.

Large outdoor gazing balls can also attract energy— not quite like a sundial, but similarly. A sundial has an attractiveness that draws a person's body because people like to study them up close. Gazing balls often just draw the eye. It's hard not to look at them—they're bright and noticeable. They've been used in gardens for centuries—they had bling before "bling" was a word. For attracting energy, a gazing ball can be any color. For reflecting energy, the ball should be silver, like a standard mirror. When using a gazing ball to

The reflective brightness of silvered glass gazing balls draws the eye and pulls chi energy to that area. The balls are available in several metallic colors.

attract energy, you need not say anything—the solution is a real cure; you have actually added something attention-grabbing. When reflecting energy back, you should say your intention out loud.

Glazed pottery is a maintenance-free way to bring unfading color into a landscape. In addition to sculptures and garden stools, there's also the ever-popular glazed pot. The big question is: Do they need a plant in them or can they just sit out, looking pretty? Decorative pots in your garden shouldn't *all* be empty. An empty pot *can* say, "I'm ready to accept bounty." But too many empty pots can say, "Empty— there's nothing here." A pot with a chip or crack is not necessarily a problem. Foliage can grow over it. Pottery shards that have been formed into other mosaic objects, such as stepping stones or tabletops, are okay, but having a collection of pottery shards outdoors in your yard is a very bad idea. It screams, "Broken things in my life!" If you store pottery shards for future craft use, do so in a labeled box in a shed.

Avoid placing bright, noticeable things down low,

around the foundation of an upraised home. By attracting the eye there, you are actually pulling energy *under* the home. Emphasizing that low energy below the home isn't good for the home in general. If you want to put objects in those locations, they should be subdued objects. Ditto for plants that are hard to resist looking at, like croton. Don't put attractive plants low around an upraised house anywhere except the entrance (to emphasize the entrance). If you intend to let a bright plant grow tall, it's okay—this only applies to plants that are *kept* low.

In Hawaiian culture and in feng shui, stones have energy and life. Treat pohaku respectfully—especially *large* smooth stones. It is inharmonious to place a smooth stone directly next to a jagged stone. In fact, sharply jagged stones are not generally recommended in gardens. In a garden, free-standing stones can represent mountains or islands, depending on what is at the base of the stone. If grass or a very low ground cover surrounds the base, it represents an island. If the base of the stone is hidden in shrubbery, it represents a mountain—

and the shrubbery represents ancient trees. To enhance that look, you may want to learn how to prune those shrubs niwaki-style. *See Recommended Reading, Chinese and Asian Gardening, pages 189-190.*

Top left: The main function of pots in feng shui is to contain and hold energy. Here, all the energy would flow to the beautiful view, but the color of the pot draws our attention, holding some of our attentive energy. A potted plant looks best when the height of the pot is one third of the height from the ground to the top of the plant, so this pot really should have a larger plant.

Top middle: The pot on the right blends in nicely so serenity is maintained. The blue pot at the far end stops the energy from running off the end of the lānai.

Top right: The bright container garden has a balanced feel when seen with the lovely blue pot.

Left: Stones that are somewhat buried feel more stable than stones just lying on the ground.

Broken Objects

It's best to avoid keeping broken statuary of people or animals. Especially problematic are statues with missing body parts. If you can't bear to get rid of it, put a dot of red paint on the place where it's broken and say out loud, "You're not broken—you're whole. No broken energy comes to my property." Then do your best to obscure the broken part with greenery or something else decorative. You don't want a constant view of something broken when looking at your garden.

Beware of storing any broken things, including vehicles, on your property. The problem is that you are unintentionally asking for something to "not work" in your life. If it's appropriate to remove the broken item, do so. If not, put a red dot on the item, and say out loud, "You're fixed." You are using the symbolism of red blood, meaning a new beginning. If you have a beautiful glazed pot with a chip or crack, but it is still useful, discreetly put a dot of red paint on the broken area, and arrange the plants so the damage isn't noticed.

Occasionally, someone will have an old stone wall on their property, a part of which is significantly damaged, perhaps by a bulldozer. It may not be possible to repair the wall for various reasons, including archeological integrity. In that case, take red thread or string and attach it to one part of the wall, string it across the broken part, and attach it to the next unbroken part. Say out loud, "You're a solid wall again." The thread can be hidden by dirt or plants. This can also be done when there's an obvious gap in a line of trees or shrubs. I consulted at a home that had a beautiful line of koa trees at the back of the property, on the makai side. The trees were in a perfect location and felt protective. But one tree was missing, and energy was leaking through the gap. I recommended planting another koa in the gap. It would be a long time before it filled in, though, so I suggested an interim fix: tying (very loosely) a red thread around the two trees on each side of the gap. The string would lie on the ground between the trees and be the symbolic bridge. If you do this, make sure the string is weak enough to break before it girdles the trees and leaves unsightly marks as they grow.

Opposite: Avoid having broken statuary of people or animals. Broken limbs are the worst, and a head on its own can seem too much like a severed head, which is not very welcoming.

Plant Symbolism

The more a symbol makes sense to you, the more powerful it will be for you. One culture does not have better or more powerful plant symbols than another culture. Different cultures have *different* symbols, not better or worse symbols. Chinese symbols are not better just because they are Chinese. They are excellent for people who feel an affinity with them. Choose the plant symbol or name that most resonates with your heart and common sense.

Here is a list of words and phrases related to gardens and plants and what they tend to signify in feng shui:

Remember that a living plant is much more than a

Opposite: Money Leaf
(*Dieffenbachia*)

Garden Word	Feng Shui Significance / Meaning
Lush	*Abundance*
Sparse or barren	*Scarcity*
Wild, jungle-like	*Chaotic, out-of-control*
One of this, one of that	*Scattered, solitary, disconnected*
Vines	*Clinging, possibly choking*
Epiphytes ("air plants")	*Abundance, or possibly burden, if there are too many*

metaphor. You need not assign meaning to all your garden plants. To try to do so would be fruitless. Any metaphor can only be pushed too far, and then it breaks down.

Physical Attributes

Physical form is perhaps the most important aspect of a plant to convey symbolic meaning.

Plant Form

This is one of the most useful aspects of a plant from a feng shui point of view—what is the basic shape of the plant? Does it grow up or down?

The botanical term for a hanging-down plant shape is "pendant" or "pendulous." If a plant hugs the ground, it's referred to as "prostrate." Some of the greatest Chinese consultants, such as Lin Yun, recommend that a weeping willow not be planted in the front yard. The suggestion is based on the sadness that the "weeping" plant portends—symbolically calling sadness to that home. But plants can't really weep—they don't have tear ducts. They can have a very flowing shape, like running water. That flowing shape is recommended in feng shui for helping with memories and feeling connected and satisfied. It's considered to break up stodginess and dispel envy. I don't see a problem with having a pendant or pendulous plant in the front yard, as long as you don't refer to it as weeping. I prefer to use the word flowing (or pendant) when referring to plants with dangling tendrils. The symbolism of water in the front yard, and in front of the door, can be accomplished with prostrate plants such as juniper and rosemary. From an aesthetic point of view, it's best not to mix pendant plants and plants with horizontal branches because the result can seem awkward and chaotic.

Plant List: Plants with Flowing Forms

- **Abutilon** or **Chinese Lantern** (*Abutlion ×hybridum*)—the flowers hang down, and the leaves resemble maple. 📷 *A*

- **California Pepper Tree** (*Schinus molle*)

- **Chenille Plant** (*Acalypha hispida*)—looks graceful and imparts an old-fashioned and comforting feel (📷 *B*). The red, catkin-like inflorescence hangs down in a very attractive way. *Acalypha godseffiana* has drooping leaves that are narrow and wavy—their droopiness does a great job of suggesting "dripping."

- **Fig** (*Ficus benjamina*)—also known as the weeping fig.

- **Firecracker** or **Lōkālia** (*Russelia equisetiformis*)—tolerant of drought, salt and wind

- **Fuchsia** (*Fuchsia ×hybrida*)—the Latin name refers to all ornamental fuchsias.

- **Mexican Flowing** (or Weeping) **Bamboo** (*Otatea acuminata* ssp. *aztecorum*)—has a pendant form. My favorite name for this plant is Otatea (oh-ta-TAY-a). It almost sounds Tahitian, and the plant itself looks extremely romantic. 📷 *C*

- **Mulberry** (*Morus nigra*)

- **Spanish Moss** (*Tillandsia usneoides*)—too much can make a place seem eerie, but if used with restraint, it can add lushness in an unexpected way and a bit of a carefree look. 📷 *D*

- **Weeping Willow** (*Salix babylonica*)

A

B

C

D

Prostrate plants, such as hearts-and-flowers, also have a flowing feeling. Plants with upward form add uplifting energy. *See Plant List: Upward-Shaped Plants, page 54.*

Leaf Shape

Heart-shaped leaves can mean love. Sharp, pointed leaves can mean danger. Round leaves can represent coins. Succulent leaves can represent fat, abundant coins. A twist in a leaf such as a croton can be delightful, but a very twisted leaf such as spinach panax can look deformed and be inauspicious.

Growth Habit

A vining habit is a yin habit because it flows like water. And it's complicated, different from the more yang

Left: 'Awa (kava) has beautiful, heart-shaped leaves which symbolize love.

Middle: The narrow leaves of this croton are rippled and twisted like a screw. A very rippling shape symbolizes water in feng shui, and water means wealth.

Right: Be cautious of including spinach plants in your garden; their leaves can look *too* stretched, twisted and weird.

This ficus tree has a banyan habit, which makes it very, very strong. It symbolizes strength, as does any sturdy tree. I don't recommend planting big ficus trees—their berries make them invasive. Koa is a better choice. The word "toa" means "big, strong tree" in Polynesian.

simplicity of a tree without a vine growing up it. Some vining, twining plants on your property are just fine, but don't let them comprise more than half of your garden. Otherwise the energy could be *too* yin.

Thorns have a very direct message in nature, and in feng shui, too—stay away! The larger a property is, the more thorny plants it can have without adverse effects. An adverse effect of too many thorny plants may be reluctance to venture very far into your yard. Your yard should beckon you—call you to see the beauty close up. You definitely don't want to encounter thorns on your way to that close-up view. If you feel you're not enjoying your garden as much as you'd like, it's time to remove some sharp things from your life. Dig up those thorny or prickly plants and replace them. Hawai'i has an immense variety of planting stock to choose from. Perhaps choose something fragrant to make a big statement of *inviting* where there used to be a big statement of *stay away*.

Banyan is not truly the name of any tree— it is the growth habit of several trees. The habit is to drop aerial roots, which then support the branches. They also help anchor the tree in high winds. *Ficus benghalensis* is the usual "banyan tree" in Hawai'i. It's not a good choice for gardens here because of its ultimate size, and because the birds eat the seeds and drop them into wild areas; native plants can't compete with a tree as aggressive as a banyan. A banyan habit in any tree symbolizes strength and endurance.

Young bamboo is tender and delicate, but it grows to be a durable and flexible plant. Bamboo's symbolism in feng shui includes those two qualities, making it a plant with good relationship energy.

Leaf and Flower Color
The most basic way our eyes and brains process plant color is either by noticing it or ignoring it. Some schools and practices in feng shui add more symbolism to color (such as the green Dragon and Elemental colors), but Landform School feng shui mostly sticks to the basics: notice it or don't notice it.

Top left to right: Red begonia flowers are very noticeable.

The pink is so bright in this coleus that it becomes as powerful as pure red.

When the sun shines through brilliant red ti leaves the effect is noticeable—in a very good way.

The flowers of a red clematis vine are large and very bright.

Bottom left to right: Copper leaf plant has rusty red leaves that aren't exactly bright.

The leaves of black leaf taro do look black, hence the name.

The undersides of 'New Guinea Black' ti leaves are so dark, they look black.

There is, however, the possibility of noticing something for the wrong reason—it sticks out like a sore thumb. Use color to draw the eye where you want it, but make the eye happy once it gets there.

Red is an important color in feng shui because it's so lively, bright and noticeable. It does indeed say, "Stop." All shades of red (pink, magenta, maroon, crimson, oxblood) bring that attractive energy, unless they are too dull or too dark. Healthy plants never truly produce the color black in their leaves or flowers, but they can display an *extremely* dark red color that is perceived as black.

Variegated leaves have an active energy and can be lovely, but they are not always appreciated by everyone—it depends on your visual temperament. I had a client on the Big Island whose home was surrounded by massive walls of green forest all around. This client knew plants well. Her father had been a gardener in Hollywood with movie star clients. When I mentioned that she might want to consider using some plants with variegated leaves to break up what I saw as possible monotony, she calmly said, "Variegation makes me nervous." I immediately shook her hand and said, "Congratulations for knowing that about yourself."

Use variegation purposefully and carefully. It's never

Top left to right: To me, this croton looks paint-splattered and nerve-wracking—not all variegations are equally pleasing to the eye, and they may bother some people more than others.

The yellow and green stripes on these leaves have too much contrast. It can make some people feel nervous.

Some people see this hibiscus flower as beautiful; others see it as simply odd.

Bottom left to right: White dieffenbachia leaves keep their light variegation even in the shade.

Variegated syngonium is a very manageable groundcover with white leaves even in a dark location.

This bed started out with only light-leaf ajuga. As you can see, the dark-leaf type now shows up. That indicates that the light variegation is not very strong and the plant will revert.

as serene as a plain leaf, but total serenity isn't necessarily the goal of an active feng shui garden. The balance of yin and yang should be considered. Variegated plants in shady locations often don't look their best, because they need sunlight to show off their brightest colors. Dieffenbachia (*Dieffenbachia maculata*) keeps its variegation admirably in even dark shade, as does the variegated syngonium, a groundcover. In some plants the variegation is unstable and the leaves will revert back to a solid color (usually green) over time.

Plant Names

The name of a plant is useful for identification and communication, but a plant is ever so much more than its name.

If a particular plant's name has an unpleasant connotation, but you like the actual plant, pick a different name. Some common plant names are quite negative and can subconsciously affect how we feel about the plant. There's no reason to dislike pothos (*Epipremnum pinnatum*) just because some people call it devil's ivy—other people call it a money plant. It's also called taro vine. In some places, slipper flower (*Pedilanthus tithymaloides*) is referred to as devil's walking stick or devil's backbone. Yes, pothos can get big and out-of-hand, and the stems of slipper flower zigzag in a somewhat spooky way, but neither plant has anything to do with the devil. I don't know why *Alstonia scholaris* is called devil tree—

it's a perfectly wonderful plant with a nicely fragrant flowers. Mother-in-law's tongue is a rude name for *Sansevieria trifasciata* and it's as many syllables as "san-sa-VER-e-uh." There is always an alternative to a negative plant name. It's a small but real way to choose positivity in your life.

Left: Pothos gets quite big and has big leaves. Don't let the negative name "devil's ivy" deter you from it. It's also called taro vine.

Alternate names abound. Check reference books and online, or ask nursery staff. Sometimes the botanical name is melodious and lovely (like carissa, for Natal plum), though not always. Botanical names can often be intimidating and cumbersome. The Hawaiian plant name is usually melodious and lovely. Using the Hawaiian plant name enlarges our vocabulary and helps keep the language alive. You can use a name from any culture that you know of, or you can invent your own name for the plant. When using the botanical name, feel free to use the genus name (the first name, capitalized when used with the species name) or the species name (the second name, uncapitalized) alone.

Right: Slipper flower is quite lovely despite being called "devil's backbone."

There are several very different plants that have "money" in their common name, or are thought of as related to money in different cultures.

Plant List: Plants Related to Money

- **Jade Plant** (*Crassula ovata*)—perhaps the most common "money plant" in feng shui. It's the one I recommend the most because of its fat leaves (which say abundance) and because it's easy to grow and stays manageable. 📷*A*

- **Malabar Chestnut** (*Pachira aquatica*)—commonly called money tree by many who practice feng shui because the five leaves are seen to symbolize an auspicious balance of the Five Chinese Elements. This plant is often grown in small pots (📷*B1*) with several trunks braided together, but it can become a large tree when planted in the ground📷 *B2*). The nuts are edible and tasty when cooked.

- **Moneywort** (*Lysimachia nummulariai*)—has round, shiny leaves the size of a nickel and can be used as a groundcover in wet areas.

continued on next page

Plant List: Plants Related to Money
continued

- **Money Tree** (*Dracaena marginata*)—first planted in Hawai'i outside the Bishop Bank in Hilo in the 1920s when the bank moved to 130 Kamehameha Avenue (into a Dickey-designed building where the Pacific Tsunami Museum is today), so in Hawai'i it's called a money tree (it's not associated with money elsewhere). It also comes in a variegated type (📷 *C*, right). The feng shui uses for this plant, at the back and sides of the property, generally relate to upwardness because its form is often upward. It should not be planted close to your home or in your front yard. *See sidebar.*

- **Philodendron scandens**—has a heart-shaped leaf and is related to money in some schools of feng shui.

- **Pothos** (*Epipremnum pinnatum*) or Golden Pothos (*E. aureum*)—related to money in some schools of feng shui, probably because of the leaves' size.

  Silver Dollar (*Lunaria annua*)—also called money plant, dollar plant and honesty.

A

B1

B2

C

KEEP MONEY UNDER CONTROL

MONEY TREE HAS NO FENG SHUI USE IN A FRONT YARD OR CLOSE TO A HOUSE, THOUGH THAT IS WHERE IT IS MOST COMMONLY FOUND. THIS PLANT CAN START SMALL, BUT IT HAS NO REASON TO EVER STOP—I'VE SEEN IT RIPPING UP SIDEWALKS AND INTERFERING WITH ROOFS AND GUTTERS. IF YOU HAVE A LARGE ONE IN THE WRONG PLACE, I RECOMMEND YOU CUT IT CLOSE TO THE GROUND AND COVER THE STUMP WITH CARDBOARD, BLACK PLASTIC AND MORE CARDBOARD. MULCH NICELY OVER THE TOP AND CAP IT OFF WITH SOMETHING ATTRACTIVE LIKE A FOUNTAIN—OR MAYBE A STATEMENT PLANT SUCH AS VARIEGATED DWARF SCHEFFLERA (*SCHEFFLERA ARBORICOLA*) IN A BEAUTIFUL POT.

Feng shui author Lillian Too mentions silver crown (*Cotyledon undulata*) as a "good fortune" plant and recommends it indoors and out. But the plant that looks the most like money to me is dieffenbachia—the type with leaves that look like big dollar bills.

Most people are familiar with lucky bamboo (*Dracaena*

REAL BAMBOO

HOW TO RECOGNIZE REAL BAMBOO: BAMBOO *NEVER* HAS LEAVES GROWING DIRECTLY OUT OF THE MAIN UPWARD STALK.

Left: Real bamboo, like this, is a grass. Its leaves never sprout from the sides of the main stem.

Middle: You can tell lucky bamboo is an imitation bamboo because the leaves grow directly from the center stalk.

Right: The leaves of bamboo palm grow directly from the center trunk.

sanderiana). It's not actually a bamboo—it just looks similar, as do many plants. The only reason it's "lucky" is because you can't kill it unless it is completely submerged in water, though it is sometimes sold that way. In most places it's an indoor houseplant, but in Hawai'i it makes an easy-to-grow garden plant as well.

Chinese Symbols

Chinese plant symbolism has many layers and many nuances. Often, a particular combination of plants (at a certain time) has a specific meaning. A list of Chinese plant symbols may not be very useful in Hawai'i, unless you have Chinese ancestors and your own intuition resonates with the appropriateness of the symbolism. With that in mind,

Plant List: Chinese Symbolic Plants

- **Bamboo**—Endurance and longevity
- **Chrysanthemum**—depending on the time and conditions, chrysanthemums may symbolize a number of things: Reclusiveness (in the late fall), modesty, nobility, longevity, gentility, a comfortable happy life.
- **Fuchsia**—Good fortune
- **Gardenia**—Good fortune
- **Jade Plant**—Abundance and prosperity
- **Japanese Apricot**—Noble traits and hardiness
- **Lotus**—Truth, purity, nobility
- **Magnolia**—Purity and truth
- **Orange**—Good fortune, wealth and happiness
- **Orchid**—Refinement, delicacy, nobility, sincerity and charm in seclusion
- **Osmanthus**—Good fortune in literary endeavors, as well as job advancement in your career
- **Peony**—Good fortune, wealth, honor, happiness and even love. In China, it is the king of flowers, but peonies won't grow in Hawai'i; they need colder weather.
- **Pine**—Longevity
- **Plum**—Purity and longevity; also friendship

WATER LILY OR LOTUS

The flower on the left is a water lily, while the one on the right is a lotus.

HOW TO RECOGNIZE LOTUS: THE SUREST WAY TO TELL IS BY THE FLOWER'S CENTER—THE LOTUS HAS ONE BIG HARD POD IN THE MIDDLE. IF THE FLOWER HAS MANY PISTILS AND STAMENS IN THE MIDDLE, IT'S A WATER LILY, WHICH HAS NONE OF THE SYMBOLISM OF A LOTUS. THE LEAVES AND FLOWERS OF LOTUS NEVER SIT DIRECTLY ON THE SURFACE OF THE WATER, AS THOSE OF A WATER LILY OFTEN DO. STANDING ABOVE THE WATER GIVES THE TRUE LOTUS ITS SYMBOLISM OF PURITY AND, IN BUDDHISM, ENLIGHTENMENT. THAT'S THE SIGNIFICANCE OF THE HARD POD IN THE MIDDLE OF THE LOTUS—IT'S WHERE THE BUDDHA OR BODHISATTVA SITS OR STANDS. WATER LILIES ARE COMMON IN HAWAI'I, WHILE LOTUS ARE RATHER UNUSUAL.

Yin and Yang

Yin and yang are among the most commonly used feng shui concepts. Water and fire are common examples of yin/yang opposites. Fire goes up like a flame and water flows out horizontally, like the horizon of the ocean.

On the next page is a yin/yang chart. Neither side represents the ideal; it's about balance—not too much one way or the other.

If an area is too yin because it's too wet and shady (and you aren't able to remedy that), add white-leafed plants like dieffenbachia or kukui. Yellow plants are almost as bright and yang as white plants. (*See Plant List: Yellow-Leafed Plants, page 97; and Plant List: Yellow-Flowering Plants, page 98.*) By all means, don't make matters worse by adding ornaments.

If part of a yard feels too open and bare, add a statue that serves as a visual affirmation of the state you aspire to— peaceful, compassionate, helpful. Choose a big statue—almost over-scale. You could also ground energy in an overexposed area by using plants with dark purple leaves. If an area was out of balance before, it should feel *transformed* when you've installed the changes.

Opposite: Kukui is a plant of light in both Hawaiian culture and in feng shui. Its powdery white leaf surface stands out and is noticeable without being brash.

Top left: The stems of this taro are quite dark and the leaves are somewhat dark.

Top right: Some joyweeds are bright yellow and red, but this one is a dark red.

Bottom left: This dark-leafed plant is purple tradescantia (*Tradescantia pallida*); it's closely related to purple wandering jew (honohono ʻula).

Bottom right: The narrow liriope leaves are so dark they are almost black.

Certain areas of Hawai'i are hammered by wind on a daily basis. Heavier individuals often find the wind refreshing, but slender people are put off-balance by constant wind. The results can vary from irritation and exhaustion to apathy and depression. The feng shui interpretation of a home situated in a very windy area is that the good fortune (including money) is blowing away. Moving is the ultimate solution, but windbreaks are cheaper, so start planting.

Plant List: Windbreak Plants

- **Alahe'ē** (*Psydrax odorata*)—native, fragrant, drought- and salt-tolerant.
- **Be-Still** (*Thevetia peruviana*) and **Oleander** (*Nerium oleander*)—both will stand up to winds and be-still makes a lovely hedge where few other plants would survive, but, as I've said before, they are quite poisonous. 📷 *A*
- **Beefsteak Plant** (*Acalypha godseffiana*)—several different plants in Hawai'i have this common name—this one reaches 10 feet.
- **Blue Vitex** (*Vitex trifolia*)
- **Ironwood** (*Casuarina equisetifolia*)—an old standard; it accepts pruning.

A

A good pamphlet, *Trees and Shrubs for Windbreaks in Hawai'i* (University of Hawai'i College of Tropical Agriculture and Human Resources, 1982), is available for free download at the UH CTAHR website. *See Resources, page 196.* The most thorough list of windbreak plants for Hawai'i is found in *Small Trees for the Tropical Landscape* by Rauch and Weissich. *See Recommended Reading.*

In windy areas, a quiet outside haven can become an oasis for your spirit. Feel free to make it complicated and interesting—but keep it clutter-free and decorate only with plants.

If you have big-leaf plants like bananas in a wind-whipped area, avoid planting them in view of the house windows or along the approach to the property. A constant view of big shredded leaves can create a frantic feel in some people. In windy areas, use plants with leaves that won't shred along the public front areas, and anywhere in view from inside the house.

Wildlife

In feng shui, birds have a heavenly connection. They are links between Heaven and Earth. I sense this when I listen to a leiothrix (also called Peking or Chinese nightingale) or the sweet song of a white-rumped shama.

However, I must use effort to remember birds' sacred role when I hear mynahs squawking. Bird feathers were honored in old Hawai'i and in old China. If you find a feather on your property, place it outside near a doorway so its good influence can help to protect the area. If birds repeatedly fly into the glass of your windows, find a way to prevent them from doing that. Place stickers on the window or add shiny moving objects, such as strips of metallic plastic.

Trees and shrubs make life possible for land birds. Before people arrived here, these islands were covered with trees and many kinds of birds and tree snails—more than there are today. The Hawaiian Islands need the return of tall trees to provide habitat for birds and the Hawaiian hoary bat, Hawai'i's only endemic land mammal. Other native wildlife, such as tree snails and insects, also need that high habitation. Nature, with a variety of life, extends hundreds of feet higher in the air than people usually realize. Trees create rain by acting as mist nets, catching moisture that would otherwise blow on by. Trees create a very positive ecological cycle, and without them no wildlife would exist. Even if a tree is dead, a pueo (owl) or an 'io (hawk) can alight there.

Feng shui looks to nature to guide the way, so native Hawaiian trees are ideal to plant. Feral ungulates (pigs, cows, goats, deer, etc.) prevent native forests from regrowing. Ungulates did not evolve on islands and should not be allowed to run wild in Hawai'i, because of the havoc they wreak upon the native plant and bird life. In addition to native trees, it's important to plant trees that bear food so that the symbolic abundance of the green foliage can become real abundance in our stomachs.

Butterflies have lively chi energy and add a unique delight to a garden. While Hawai'i has over a thousand species of native moths, there are only two native butterflies.

Left: Māmaki is the host plant for the native Kamehameha Butterfly. There are only two native butterflies in Hawai'i.

Right: Koa is the host plant for Blackburn's Blue, the other native Hawaiian butterfly.

To attract these lovely creatures, cultivate their host plants. The Kamehameha Butterfly likes māmaki (*Pipturus albida*), and the Blackburn's Blue generally goes for koa (*Acacia koa*). Other plants attract non-native butterflies.

A

Plant List: Plants to Attract Butterflies

- **Butterfly Bush** (*Buddleia davidii*)—these are available in several colors including a deep purple, 'Black Knight.'

- **Crownflower** (*Calotropis gigantean*)—also called pua kalaunu. It's very easy to grow, especially in hot, dry areas. It even tolerates salt spray.

- **Pentas** (*Pentas lanceolata*)—blooms year-round and is available in several colors, commonly red, white or pink. The pink pentas pictured came from the seeds of red pentas. Eventually, the new generations may become white; the red color is not always a strong genetic trait in this flower. 📷 *A*

That which is native is that which is greatest, when it comes to the animals that live in Hawai'i (or any island ecosystem). The species that were here before any people arrived are the kupuna (elder) species. Protect them—they are the most precious chi energy. If you have them on your property, don't disturb their habitat unnecessarily.

Maintenance

The pictures in this book are of *moments* in time, but actual gardens are *about* time. Gardens require maintenance because their positive energy comes from living plants. Where there is life, there is change. With growth and change, old leaves drop and die, and along come microorganisms—tiny wonderful chi energy—returning nutrients to the soil. They are a very yin type of life, but without them the circle of life is not complete.

Palm fronds should not be removed as long as they have any green color left. If you're concerned about fronds falling, plant shorter palms such as dwarf coconut palms. A too-perfect landscape isn't the goal in feng shui. Nature is never too perfect. There's always a bit of entropy going on. Something's dying somewhere. It's part of the balance, and it is not necessary to hide natural cycles. If resort-style landscaping is your goal, I urge you to rethink it. A Hollywood fantasy or dream paradise is, by definition, false. However, don't use that as an excuse to go overboard the other way—trash and junk cars in the front yard will not attract good energy for you or your family, guaranteed.

Messy Tree?

Some people call certain trees "messy." There's a peaceful, natural feeling under this jacaranda, but it makes some people want to get out a leaf blower. Don't. Leaf blowers upset the peaceful energy near the soil. It's best to avoid using them on your property. Be aware of whether fallen leaves or flowers in your yard disturb you subconsciously. If they've fallen on a natural area and don't bother you, you can live with nature's way. Leaf mulch encourages beneficial microorganisms in moist—but not waterlogged—soil. If fallen leaves are not for you, rake or sweep peacefully, knowing that the gorgeous tree is worth a bit of extra yardwork.

If your lawn is flat and level enough, use an old-fashioned non-gas mower to preserve a peaceful energy near the body of the Earth, the 'āina. Loud, gas-powered equipment should only be used after ruling out quieter alternatives, such as rakes or a groundcover instead of a lawn. If you have hired help with maintenance, make sure they know what to mow and what not to mow. I've seen liriope (*Liriope muscari*) that had been mowed like grass, to awkward results. Don't ever mow liriope or mondo grass (*Ophiopogon japonicus*); they are not true grasses and will not grow back well.

Top: Liriope is kept well away from the paving stones; even though the leaves are harmless, they have a pointed appearance.

Middle: Mondo is not a true grass and should never be mowed.

Bottom: A treehouse can encourage children to spend more time outdoors.

Children belong outdoors, instead of always in front of televisions and computers. Have your children or grandchildren help with yard and garden maintenance. They will thank you later after they realize the value of an ingrained work ethic and a habit of useful physical exercise. In future years, their spouses will be grateful for the gardening skills they can continue to pass on.

"First they sleep, then they creep, then they leap," a common saying goes, in reference to the growth of tropical plants. Sometimes each of the first two phases lasts a year; then suddenly, they leap for the rest of their lives. Be akamai (knowledgeable) about the eventual size of a plant before planting it near your house. **Do not allow plant leaves to touch the outside of your home.** They have a stifling effect, and they are bad for the physical health of the building. Anything that is bad for the home structure is bad feng shui. Plants may touch outside stairs and lānai, but not the "skin" of your house.

Left; This 'Janet Craig' dracaena is planted too close to the house. If plant leaves are touching your house, it's time to prune.

Right: This jade vine has grown too close to the house and should be cut back—way back.

Just because you can use a saw doesn't mean you should start hacking away—certainly not without a good understanding of how plants respond to trimming. Prune correctly; do not leave stubs. I feel it's a good idea to give the plants verbal warning before cutting, either days in advance or just before you cut. Say out loud something like, "You're going to be pruned, and I will try to see to it that the cutting is done in such a way that you can recover well." It doesn't matter exactly what you say as long as you inform the plant you mean it no harm.

'Ulu is breadfruit— the once and future plant. Keep it pruned low and harvestable to enjoy the fruit as well as the lovely leaf shape.

Part of pruning correctly is knowing *when* to prune. For many trees, it makes a huge difference. For instance, if you prune 'ulu in the wet season, it's more likely to introduce rot into the tree. Mango pruning should be done before a flush of new growth occurs. This happens several times a year; one of those times occurs immediately following the fruiting season.

If you have a lot of root-bound plants in pots on your property, that will affect your life, and not in a good way. A root-bound plant has reached its limit. It needs a larger pot, or root pruning and nutrition. A neglected plant will become obvious. When the plants start showing signs that they're poorly cared for, they become clutter. Clutter has the ability to nag you, both consciously and subconsciously. You may not even notice it because you are so accustomed to the sight. It's easy for plants kept in their original plastic pot from the nursery to become root-bound; they cry out, "Do something to help me!" Rescue your root-bound plants so you can feel more peaceful, expand your own roots and no longer be stifled.

Don't keep too many potted plants if you don't have a system to take good care of all of them. Only nurseries should have lots of plants in black plastic pots. Don't let a plant put roots through the bottom of the plastic pot. If this has already happened and you want to keep the plant where it is, cut away the plastic pot and mound dirt around the roots. Plant something to obscure the mound, so that only the upper part of the plant is in view.

The leaves of some plants (like coleus) go limp during the heat of the day but perk up again later. If you notice your plants are continually limp from lack of water, adjust your watering habits or plant something more drought-tolerant.

Removing a dead or dying tree is often seen as showing disrespect for the spirit of the tree or another spirit that may be lodged in the tree. A spirit in a tree is believed to be common in very old trees, and trees in remote places. If there is a dead tree on your property, the most natural solution is to plant a vine around it. The tree continues to have purpose as a perch for birds. This applies only to dead trees that are still firmly rooted with no threat of falling branches. Any of the vines listed on page 70-71 is up to the task of changing the look of dead branches into stunning blossoms.

A dead tree can be a perch for birds and a support for vines. This brings life to that upward space.

Electromagnetic Fields (EMFs)

Electromagnetic fields (EMFs) are not usually a concern in yards and gardens unless there are electric substations, power transformers, large electric wires or microwave receivers nearby. If you have any of those close by, I recommend that you measure the EMFs with a gaussmeter. (Gauss is the measurement of magnetism.) If you can't find someone who already has a meter, you can order one through AlphaLab Inc. (*See Resources, page 194.*) Less expensive gaussmeters are available at online retailers for as little as $20.

Hopefully, measuring EMF levels in your home will reassure you that there is no concern. If, however, the EMF level is high, here are some possible scenarios:

• The EMFs are high only in a specific area where no one spends any significant amount of time. Don't worry about it.

• The EMFs are rather high throughout areas where someone spends a good deal of time. Sadly, there's not much you can do about it. As far as I know, a wall of metal is the only thing that stops EMFs in the frequencies of most concern. I'd be especially concerned about the situation if children played there, children being more susceptible to EMF damage. Try to reduce the time spent in these areas.

• If the EMFs are quite high, as for example, from an electric substation next door—move! I realize this is a radical suggestion, but I'm very serious. Luckily, high levels of EMFs are rare in Hawai'i gardens. 🍃

SPECIAL GARDENS

Your garden may have a specific purpose or style, and often the physical constraints of your home's location will impact the type of garden you are able to cultivate. Be it humble or grand, your garden can do wonders for your life.

Food

Food gardens symbolize abundance because they truly are a literal source of abundance. Food gardens provide exercise and better nourishment and help sustain the planet. They are auspicious anywhere, and the bigger the better. Situate them for the best sun. (Ours is in the front yard.) Food gardens require care, but that's the message that goes out into the neighborhood—that you care enough to make food production a priority. If you've got a food garden, be proud of it!

Feng shui derives from nature, and the best feng shui works *with* nature, using organic methods rather than chemicals. Herbicide use is very popular in Hawai'i, resulting in dead areas that look scorched—that's not good feng shui. If you must use weed killers, be sure to remove all dead plants afterwards.

For life above the soil, there must be life below the soil— and the more life, the better, from a feng shui point of view. Biochar is pure charcoal—no chemicals added to help it burn in a grill. Once the biochar has been inoculated with microorganisms and dug into the soil, it can cut your use of fertilizers in half. The charcoal pieces are fairly small, but not powder-fine. Just as fermented foods like poi add healthful microorganisms to our bodies, the charcoal, with microorganisms living on its many tiny surfaces, adds them to the soil. Soil teeming with microbes supports healthy plants. *See Resources, page 195.*

Food is beautiful— be proud of it. Tend your vegetable beds well and reap the abundance.

GMO (genetically-modified organism) plants are the antithesis of good feng shui. Nature has been left left far behind in that technology. As Marcia Bjornerud says in *The Autobiography of the Earth*, "The belief that we can engineer what evolution has done in four billion years—and expect the results to be predictable and controllable—is a sign of our youth and ignorance."

Hybrid seeds are acceptable because they're not far removed from natural cross-breeding. They may not be good for seed-saving though, because the new keiki plants don't generally have the qualities of the parent plant. I mostly use non-hybrid seeds in our vegetable garden. It's very easy to save seeds from our own vegetables and replant. A quick replanting of seeds from your own peppers (capsicum, not pepper spice) or pole beans germinates almost instantly.

I'm very grateful for my hybrid Jersey King asparagus, which produces well in Hawai'i. We grew it from male crown starts. If we grew from seed we'd have a mixture of male and female plants. Only the female plants produce seeds, and they are plentiful, like weeds. By the way, asparagus and coconut appreciate a big drink of seawater every so often; they both evolved around it.

I'm a great believer in edible landscaping—food looks beautiful to me. Edible plants can be used for any of the plant solutions that are mentioned in this book. Here are some that are useful to lift energy upward where the ground slopes down and away from the house at the back or sides.

Plant List: Upward Edible Plants

- **Bamboo**—many species are edible. *Nastus elatus* is the only one that's delicious raw.

- **Palm**—"heart of palm" refers to the edible inner core of several types of palm, including coconut. *Bactris gasipaes* is called peach palm, and it's a bunching palm, which means you won't kill the whole tree when you harvest the core. The fruit, called a drupe, is also edible. (📷*A1*) Açaí palm (*Euterpe oleracea*) can create an upward feel and look tropical—plus, the fruit is edible and very nutritious. (📷*A2*) Date palms (*Phoenix dactylifera*) produce well in Hawai'i if you're in a very dry area (like Kawaihae on the Big Island).

Plant List: Upward Edible Plants

• **Pandan** (*Pandanus amaryllifolus*, sometimes classified as *P. odorus*)—also called sweet or fragrant pandan and related to hala (*Pandanus tectorius*). It is a lovely, easy-to-grow upward plant. I recommend this plant for all homes that cook rice. Put one or two leaves into the rice as it starts to cook. Your kitchen will instantly smell like comfort food. Remove the leaves before serving. 📷 *B*

• **Papaya** (*Carica papaya*)—zooms up faster than most plants and grows easily from fresh seed, although commercially sold seeds are less likely to have GMO contamination. (📷 *C1*) These clone papayas (📷 *C2*) are non-GMO and were purchased from Agri-Starts (*see Resources*). Harvesting is a breeze because they start bearing extremely low.

• **Pepper** (*Capsicum* spp.)—see sidebar.

• **Pineapple** (*Ananas comosus*)—not all the leaves point up, but overall there is a strong upward feel. 📷 *D*

A1   A2   B

C1   C2   D

PICK A PEPPER

SOME KINDS OF GARDEN PEPPERS HOLD THEIR FRUIT DOWN AND SOME HOLD IT UP. THIS BIRD PEPPER (LEFT) HOLDS ITS FRUIT UP AND THEREFORE LIFTS ENERGY. IT IS ALSO SUITABLE FOR THE FRONT YARD TO REPRESENT THE RED BIRD. NOTE THAT BLACK PEPPER (*PIPER NIGRUM*, RIGHT), THE SPICE, IS AN ENTIRELY DIFFERENT PLANT. BLACK PEPPER IS RELATED TO 'AWA AND GROWS WELL IN HAWAI'I IF IT GETS ENOUGH WATER AND A PLACE TO CLIMB, SUCH AS HĀPU'U STUMPS.

Katuk makes a fine hedge plant, and the leaves are wonderful cooked greens.

If you need to screen harsh energy from view, fruit trees will do the job. Most fruit trees are best kept low so that the fruit can be easily harvested. This includes mango, 'ulu, jaboticaba, citrus and Surinam cherry. The flavor of the dark-fruited Surinam cherry is preferred by many people. Some fruit trees, such as avocado, don't make the best screens because they drop most of their leaves once a year. There are also hedge plants with edible leaves, such as chaya (*Cnidoscolus chayamansa*), which is also called tree spinach, and katuk (*Sauropus androgynus*). The leaves of both plants should be eaten cooked, not raw.

Not everyone wants or can have trees, but there are several edible plants that can climb trellises or dead trees, providing other screening options.

Plant List: Edible Climbing Plants for Screening

- **Chayote** or **Pīpīnola** (*Sechium edule*)—can create a lush green screen very quickly. 📷*A*
- **Kabocha** or **Japanese Pumpkin** (*Curcurbita moschata*)—the leaves are large and the squash is delicious. It can be trained up a trellis but often does best growing along the ground where it can re-root. 📷*B*
- **Liliko'i** (*Passiflora edulis*)
- **Pole Beans** (*Phaseolus vulgaris*)—usually last only a few months, but lima beans can produce for several years.
- **Vanilla** (*Vanilla planifolia*)

A

B

Left: This amazing liliko'i pergola was created simply by propping up the vine as it grew to create a canopy. T-top crossbars are screwed into the support posts. It looks gorgeous whether viewed from outside or within, and fruit is easily harvested.

Many edible plants have rounded leaves and are suitable for welcoming energy at the front of your property.

Plant List: Edible Plants with Rounded Leaves

- **Collards** (*Brassica oleracea* var. *acephala*)—an acquired taste for some people, but so is poi. Collards are one of the most nutritious foods on the planet, and in Hawai'i they're perennial. The leaves are beautifully rounded. As the plant grows it flops over and more branches start along the now-horizontal stem. 📷 *A*

- **Herbs**—sage (*Salvia officinalis*), oregano (*Oreganum vulgare*), marjoram and the mints (*mentha* spp.) are excellent choices. Sage (📷 *B*) has very rounded leaves and is therefore a welcoming plant. It is also available with interesting variegated or beautiful purple leaves.

- **Lettuce** (*Lactuca sativa*)

- **Purslane** (*Portulaca oleracea*)—has nice fat leaves and grows easily, maybe a little too easily.

A   B

If you are a food gardener, you will probably meet more food gardeners. That in itself is a blessing, because food gardeners tend to be very nice people. Some islands have seed exchanges in various districts. If there's one in your area, join in and share your garden's seeds and starts—if there isn't, consider organizing one.

Teach your children to love spending time outside and to appreciate nature. It's good for a child's chores to include yard work. At pre-school age, I started helping in my grandmother's gigantic vegetable garden; I first dug and planted my own garden as a 4-H Club project when I was in the fourth grade. My quick, colorful success with zinnias got me hooked, and I haven't stopped since.

Wait to pick tree fruit until it is as ripe as possible, but before the birds get it. No citrus should be picked green, not even lime. Limes will turn yellow when they are ripe on the tree. The wonderful-tasting sweet lime doesn't taste like anything but water unless it is allowed to ripen on the tree to the point that it comes off in your hand when you nudge it. All citrus is like that—try to wait until all the green is gone from the skin. I often don't even need clippers when harvesting citrus. A light touch will cause the ripe ones to drop into my hand. Some areas are troubled by plant theft, and the riper a fruit gets, the more tempting it becomes. If that sort of theft plagues your neighborhood, plant the most valuable food plants closer to the house and consider fencing. If you need to get a permit to make a fence higher than usual, then do so. Mamey (*Mammea americana*) is a beautiful tree with a much sought-after fruit that can be particularly subject to theft because it looks ripe before it actually is ripe. When you scratch a ripe mamey, the skin beneath is a cinnamon color; on an unripe fruit, it's green.

The commonsense truth about poisonous plants: unless you know you can eat it, don't put it in your mouth. Some of the plants common in Hawai'i are incredibly toxic. Avoid getting plant sap into your eyes, especially white plant sap— take this very seriously.

Fragrance

Pleasant fragrances are a sure but subtle way to attract good chi energy—just as unpleasant smells repel good energy. Aroma is more diffuse than a source of light or sound, but it's important not to neglect it. Give yourself the gift of fragrance on your property. You'll truly appreciate it as you find yourself slowing down and breathing more deeply.

Fragrance should be a part of every garden near the house and outdoor living areas, along frequently used pathways and near the road as a gift to people passing by. Also, as mentioned in Chapter 3, if you have a disagreeable neighbor, plant sweetly fragrant plants along the border between your property and theirs.

Most plants with aromatic flowers have a season of bloom followed by a period of no fragrance. Cinnamon gardenia (*Tabernaemontana pachysiphon*) is a delightfully fragrant plant that blooms year-round. It is not a true gardenia and is not subject to the black sooty mold that so often plagues gardenias. With plumeria, the best fragrance is not found in the pinks. The same is true with angel's trumpet (*Brugmansia ×candida*). The pure white variety has a lovely scent which is not cloying at all.

Do not plant night-blooming jasmine (*Cestrum nocturnum*). It is quite a pest in Hawai'i because it is

Opposite: Cinnamon gardenia blooms every day of the year; not many fragrant plants do that.

Left: Pink or yellow angel's trumpet looks romantic, but the finest fragrance comes from the pure white flowers.

Right: White angel's trumpet has an excellent fragrance with no hint of cloying sweetness.

Left: Don't grow night-blooming jasmine on your property. Birds deposit the seeds from the berries, making it an extremely invasive plant in Hawai'i.

Right: The sweet or fragrant ixora is also called 'Millionaire.' Its fragrance carries on the breeze and makes you feel rich.

Plant List: Fragrant Plants
continued

- **Pakalana** (*Telosma cordata*)—the fragrance is loved by all.
- ***Philodendron giganteum***—has flowers with the unexpected and refreshing smell of wintergreen, especially in the evening. If appropriate, plant it outside your bedroom window. As the name suggests, the leaves are indeed gigantic—up to four feet long. 📷 *M1, M2*
- ***Pittosporum tobira***—flowers best at higher elevations.
- ***Pittosporum viridiflorum***
- **Plumeria** (*Plumeria* spp.)
- **Plumeria Vine** (*Chonemorpha fragrans*)—it's not related to plumeria, but the flowers look similar.
- **Pua Kenikeni** (*Fagraea berteriana*)—available in regular, large and super-large flowers. In my opinion the regular smells the best. The exquisite fragrance spreads through a garden in an enchanting way. 📷 *N*
- **Rose**—because of their thorns, roses should not be grown near pathways. A variety of very fragrant roses grow well in Hawai'i. No other flower smells like a rose. 📷 *O*
- **Spider Lily** (*Crinum asiaticum*)—has a pleasant but mild fragrance.
- ***Stemmadenia litoralis***—the flower petals have a crepe texture. Although they are beautiful, the scent is not universally loved; it's a bit soapy for some people. 📷 *P*
- **Stephanotis** (*Stephanotis floribunda*)—in addition to the great fragrance, the leaves of this vine have an elegant form and texture. 📷 *Q*
- **Sweet Ixora** (*Ixora odorata*)—commonly called Millionaire, in reference to the size of the flower balls. Pōpō lehua is the Hawaiian name for all ixoras. It has an excellent smell and can be used in a wide variety of ways in the garden—trimmed or untrimmed.
- **Sweet Olive** or **Tea Olive** (*Osmanthus frangrans*)—called kwai-fah in Chinese and usugi-mokusei in Japanese. It is not invasive (as are some olives in Hawai'i) and grows best in cool, moist areas. The flowers are tiny but their scent is powerful. It is my personal favorite fragrant flower. 📷 *R1, R2*
- **Thai Wedding Flower** (*Wrightii religiosa*)—a shrub known as swi mai in Chinese. 📷 *S*
- **Tuberose** (*Polianthes tuberose*)—a popular flower for lei. It's called kupaloke in Hawaiian.
- **Violet** or **Waioleka** (*Viola odorata*)—the sweet violet.
- **Yesterday-Today-and-Tomorrow** (*Brunfelsia australis*)—this species was formerly called *latifolia*.
- **Ylang-Ylang** (*Cananga odorata*)

A

B

C

D1

D2

D3

E1

E2

F

G1

G2

G3

H1

H2

I

J1

J2

K

L1

L2

L3

M1

M2

N

O

P

Q

R1

R2

S

Dry

Top left: Bromeliads can be useful for landscaping in dry areas, but if they have barbs along the edges of the leaves, don't plant them near entrances or pathways.

Top right and bottom: Spineless bromeliads won't cut you, and the flowers can be just as extravagant and showy as those of any other bromeliad.

Previous: The fascinating leaf variegation of spineless bromeliads makes a wonderful dry garden feature. However, the leaves appear prickly, so don't use them along paths or where people congregate.

Much of Hawai'i is dry but becomes quite lush when you "just add water." If you don't want to add the water, you can still have an abundance of plants if you xeriscape—use plants that do well without much water. Don't overdo spiky and thorny plants, and especially don't locate them close to pathways, lānai or places where people pass by or gather. They are best used anywhere the property slopes down (except the front yard). They are dramatic, but in a threatening way that is not good feng shui.

Instead, use rounded-leaf succulent plants such as jade plant and fairy crassula. *See Plant List: Succulents with Round or Rounded Leaves, page 10.*

Many bromeliads, like pineapples, have spines along the edge of their leaves, but there are many gorgeous bromeliads that have totally smooth edges without a hint of sharpness—especially guzmania. *Guzmania zamora* is well known in the garden trade and has a classic red flower. There are also several so-called "spineless" bromeliads in the tillandsia genus—Spanish moss for instance. Bromeliads do well in a wide variety of elevations and climates. All types need some sunlight, especially to produce flowers. Most bromeliads are tank plants and can breed mosquitoes in the water they hold. For that reason, many people choose not to grow them.

Lānai

I mentioned this earlier, but it bears repeating here—don't place seating directly under hanging objects such as pots. In fact, it's best to keep hanging plants to a minimum on the lānai. Balance the energy with some upward plants. The lānai is not the place for plants with thorns or leaves that are stiff and prickly, like most bromeliads. (When's the last time you were tempted to hug a pineapple?) There needs to be more space between your living area (which, in Hawai'i, tends to include the lānai) and something that can poke you. The most friendly stiff, spiky plant is *Sansevieria trifascata*, because

the points always aim up. Corn plant (*Dracaena fragrans*) is also a good choice for lānai gardens. It has an upward form, and it provides privacy.

Spanish moss is one of the most yin plants because of its extremely droopy energy, almost like water dripping. A restrained amount of Spanish moss is fine—it's the world's friendliest bromeliad—but too much can make an area seem haunted.

In a windy location, a sheltered lānai gives an opportunity to grow big-leaf plants without the wind ripping them to shreds. It can be a relief to look out at whole big leaves, especially when they would be shredded if they were growing on other parts of your property. Don't keep too many small, non-plant items as lānai decoration. The plants, with their pots or stands, should be the main decorative elements.

Creative possibilities for lānai potted plants can be found in any houseplant book. If a plant works as a houseplant in temperate climates, it will probably thrive on a lānai in

Here, lovely red Chinese stools are employed as side tables for the more comfortable lānai seating. The stools have no sharp edges to create poison arrows, and they can assert energy without being too showy.

Hawai'i. Dwarf snowbush makes a terrific potted plant—it's quite interesting and has round leaves. Be sure to have at least one fragrant plant on your lānai.

I'd like to emphasize how well a ceramic Chinese garden stool can enhance a lānai. It can serve as a table, chair or plant stand, and because it's round it doesn't create any poison arrows.

Courtyard

Any principles effective for lānai gardens (previous section) apply to courtyards as well. Courtyards provide privacy and escape from the wind. If you would like your courtyard to be more private from mauka neighbors, consider a pergola that supports a vine. The quieter air of the courtyard can be soothing—and hopefully doest not harbor too many mosquitoes. Since Hawai'i's mosquitoes go to sleep at night, a courtyard or lānai can be most comfortable in the evening.

This view looks through the courtyard to another part of the home. This is a well-used courtyard—part of the living space of the home. Blue jade vine flowers provide a stunning dose of nature while protecting privacy.

Opposite: Red jade vine's canopy of leaves creates privacy, as its blossoms provide pizzazz.

Agricultural

It is often advisable to screen heavily agricultural areas—whether they are your own or belong to an adjacent or otherwise viewable property—from the house. This is especially recommended if some of the agricultural practices look awkward or unnatural, such as branches that are propped up or staked down, or a plant like coffee that is "stumped" (cut back severely) year after year. Coffee (*Coffea arabica*) will naturally grow to more than 20 feet, but we don't usually see it grown that way because it's more difficult to pick at that height.

On the other hand, if your agricultural area looks nice and natural, there's no need to screen it from the house. Looking out your windows and seeing food growing is a good thing—edible landscaping all the way! ☙

Opposite: Coffee trees are repeatedly cut down to stumps, as is cinnamon, after harvest. Any awkward agricultural practice should be screened from your window views.

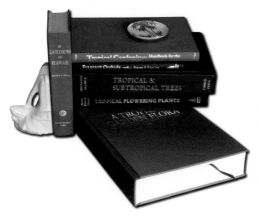

Recommended Reading

If you grow plants, you'll grow *better* plants if you learn about them, and about how they interact with animals and other plants. I believe in staying curious and continuing to expand my education, so I keep on reading. Here are some titles I recommend to extend what I touch on within this book.

Feng Shui

These resources are recommended for their in-depth content on the relationship between feng shui and the landscape:

Practical Feng Shui for the Home by Albert Low is an excellent selection of articles from his Q&A column for *The Star* in Kuala Lumpur. Low is also the author of *Feng Shui: The Way to Harmony*. No matter how much feng shui you know, you will learn a tremendous amount from this book. He covers many topics and unique situations that aren't found in other feng shui books. However, the illustrations can be confusing. Some of the questions are quite unique, and Low isn't afraid to say, "Move." (I consider "move" to be a four-letter word and try to suggest it only as an extreme last resort.)

The Art and Science of Feng Shui by Henry Lin is an extremely wise book. Lin lists 23 kinds of water with metaphorical names suggestive of their feng shui uses. He quotes extremely old sources that aren't mentioned outside of Chinese texts. He not only explains the concept of living and dead Dragon mountains; he also classifies them by their Element.

Lighting the Eye of the Dragon by Baolin Wu. Wu stresses points that other books don't cover at all—the positioning of fu dogs and lion statues (and the differences between the two), the importance of birds and feathers, and tasting the dirt. According to him, "Ancient trees can get rid of bad Qi. Some very old trees can become the seat of a personality too far removed from human energy for them to be safely approached." Wu knows feng shui to his bones—he's old school and wonderful!

Feng Shui & Your Health by Dr. Jes Lim. I can't recommend this book highly enough. I go back to it again and again— it's a very deep source of feng shui wisdom. The illustrations of positive and negative views of tree limbs (viewed from a window) are found in no other books that I know of.

Feng Shui: The Ancient Wisdom of Harmonious Living for Modern Times and *A Master Course in Feng Shui,* both by Eva Wong. She's my number-one favorite, both for her knowledge and for her husband's excellent illustrations.

Hawai'i Gardening

A Tropical Garden Flora by George Staples and Derral Herbst is the definitive word on plants grown in Hawai'i. It covers 2,100 species, but there aren't many pictures. Another excellent book, but again with no color pictures, is the encyclopedic *Permacopia* by Hunter Beyer and Franklin Martin. If I want to know whether or not a plant has potential to be weedy in Hawai'i, this is the book I turn to.

The best two books with color photography are *Tropical Ornamentals* by Arthur Whistler and *Plants for Tropical Landscapes* by Fred Rauch and Paul Weissich. The latter book is more accessible because it is arranged by the type of plant— ground cover, large tree, small shrub, etc. Rauch and Weissich are also the authors of *Small Trees for the Tropical Landscape,* which is excellent as well. The Whistler book is arranged by botanical name. It's easy enough to flip through the color pictures until you see the plant you're looking for. The cultivation information is not extensive—it's primarily useful as a great identification guide.

placement of stones. *Zen Gardens* by Tom Wright and Mizuno Katsuhiko is a small but spectacular book featuring the gardens of Kyoto. If you plan to prune your trees in a Japanese style please read *Niwaki: Pruning, Training and Shaping Trees the Japanese Way* by Jake Hobson. It includes shrubs and bamboo and has enough information to last a lifetime.

Asian food gardening is an ancient craft and can provide sustainable models. *Farmers for Twenty Centuries: Permanent Agriculture in China, Korea and Japan* by F.H. King is a classic, written in 1911. Learn how these farmers repeatedly used the same fields productively without destroying fertility or applying artificial fertilizer. Books by Masanobu Fukuoka teach a method that requires no machines, no chemicals and very little weeding. *One Straw Revolution: An Introduction to Natural Gardening* was written in 1975 and published in English in 1978. *The Natural Way of Farming* is another Fukuoka text.

Fragrance Gardening

There are numerous books on fragrance gardening. Most relevant to Hawai'i are *The Essence of Paradise* by Tovah Martin, *The Evening Garden* by Peter Loewer, *Fragrant Flowers of the South* by Eve Miranda, *Growing Fragrant Plants* by Rayford Reddell and Robert Galyean and the encyclopedic *Scented Flora of the World* by Roy Genders.

Fragrant Orchids by Steven Frowine is a must-have book for Hawai'i gardeners. Heavenly fragrance, here and now, in your own garden, can be just as easy as add-an-orchid. The book is complete and even has excellent lists: the time of day for fragrance, the season that the orchid is bloom, the intensity of fragrance and so forth. With color pictures throughout, it's beautiful as well as informative.

Nature

It's good for gardeners to have an understanding of the workings of nature. I recommend these books for deeper knowledge about the natural world. *A Forest Journey: The Role of Wood in the Development of Civilization* by John Perlin helps us understand how much we've disturbed the natural forests of the Earth. It will inspire you to reforest these islands. *The Sixth Extinction: Patterns of Life and the Future of Humankind* by Richard Leakey is excellent and well-researched. *The Song of the Dodo: Island Biogeography in an Age of Extinction* by David Quammen is of special interest—several of the sections focus on Hawai'i.

Reading the Rocks: The Autobiography of the Earth by Marcia Bjornerud is a remarkable learning experience. I find this quote sums up the scope of the work admirably: "Perhaps the greatest challenge we face in attempting to fathom the Earth is to gain a proper sense of our own size as a human species; like spoiled children, we routinely overestimate our importance on the planet but underestimate the destructiveness of our self-absorption."

Mosquito: The Story of Man's Deadliest Foe by Andrew Spielman and Michael D'Antonio is a fascinating book. You'll realize that old phrase "lucky you live Hawai'i" is especially true—there is little mosquito-borne disease in the Islands. *Animals in Translation* by Hunter Grandin changed my life. It explains how animals notice detail—without mental attachment, which is amazingly similar to how I've trained myself to notice detail in feng shui. When we see the world with a quiet mind, fresh awareness enters.

Glossary

Bagua mirror

Bagua mirrors represent perfect balance and harmony. They should not be used casually. In my own practice, I never use them to attract energy. They are the strongest solution, used in feng shui when a problem is particularly onerous. They symbolically push energy away and at the same time put things back in perfect order. A feng shui bagua mirror has specific details: eight sides decorated with the eight *I Ching* trigrams. Some feng shui consultants prefer bagua mirrors that have frames with red, green and golden colors. Be sure to peel off any protective film covering the glass when you put up the mirror.

Mirrors with a concave shape are often recommended for outside the home because of their ability to "shrink" problems. In a concave mirror a distant image looks very small. When some feng shui professionals recommend bagua mirrors for outside use, they recommend the concave kind almost exclusively. There are also many uses for convex bagua mirrors, such as to push back the busy energy of a highway or the ocean. *See also: Resources, page 194.*

Chi energy

"Chi" refers to energy—of any kind. It's also spelled "qi" in Pinyin and "ki" in Japanese. If chi is negative or harsh, it's called sha chi or shar chi.

Endemic plants

Plants that evolved in one specific place on Earth and are not naturally found anywhere else. Hawai'i's endemic plants are quite endangered and should be given preference if you can grow them in your area.

Indigenous plants

Plants that arrived without the aid of humans, but which also grow elsewhere. They do not include the 24 or so "canoe plants" (such as breadfruit, ti and 'awa) that came with the Polynesian settlers.

Native plants

This category includes both the endemic and indigenous plants of Hawai'i. It is a loose term and can include the "canoe plants."

Seal of Solomon mirror

A mirror with the traditional symbol of two equilateral triangles: it represents perfect balance. It can feel more appropriate culturally to some people than a bagua mirror and can be used anytime a bagua mirror is called for. It should not be used as a decorative item; it has a specific function—protection. One of the virtues of these mirrors is that you can make one yourself by using tape or scratching the glass surface—just be sure to get the proportions correct. *See Resources* for a Hawai'i source for lovely stained-glass models. The use of Seal of Solomon mirrors is innovative in feng shui. For more information on this, read *Feng Shui & Your Health* by Jes Lim. *See Recommended Reading, page 187.*

Seal of Solomon mirror

Yin/Yang

A system of dividing energy (chi) into two categories, the ideal situation being neither totally yang nor completely yin, but rather in perfect balance. This system is discussed in *Primitive Classification* by Durkheim and Mauss, who say, "Such classifications are thus intended, above all, to connect ideas, to unify knowledge; as such, they may be said without inexactitude to be scientific, and to constitute a first philosophy of nature." *See Yin/Yang Chart, page 144.*

Resources

Bagua mirrors are available at these two stores in Chinatown: Dragon Gate Bookstore in the Chinese Cultural Plaza, 100 N. Beretania St., Honolulu, HI 96817, 808-533-7147, emilyng@hawaii.rr.com; and Feng Shui Art & Gifts, 1120 Maunakea St., #181, Honolulu, HI 96817, 808-533-7092, teahutllc@yahoo.com.

Cloned plant keiki are available are available from Agri-Starts, Inc., agristarts.com

Concrete statuary and fountains are available at Popopots, 808-680-7676, popopots.com

Door mats with a beautiful Hawaiian quilt pattern in red against a black background are available from Tutuvi Sitoa, 2636 S. King St. (on the mauka side near University), Honolulu, HI 96826, 808-949-4355.

Exceptional garden ornaments of art quality can be found at Volcano Garden Arts, 808-985-8979, volcanogardenarts.com. Another source on the Big Island is Garden Inspirations, 808-326-9392.

Gaussmeters start at around $30, plus shipping, from online shopping sites. My personal gaussmeter is a more expensive model that also measures microwaves, purchased from trifield.com.

Glow-in-the-dark planters are available at rotoluxe.com.

Permeable paving systems are detailed at pavingexpert.com/grasspav.htm.

Red pots are available at Tropical Garden Accents, 808-259-9851, tgaccents.com.

Seal of Solomon mirror designed by Dianne McMillen, available through Lavender Moon Gallery, 79-7404 Māmalahoa Highway, Kealakekua, HI 96750, 808-324-7708, lavendermoongallery.com. (Located on the Big Island in Kainaliu, near Oshima's.)

Vetiver grass information is available at vetiverfarmshawaii.com.

Gardening help lines

Here are some times and numbers for gardening help lines at the University of Hawai'i Cooperative Extension Service. Please call the number for your island.

- O'ahu: "Master Gardener" Hotline, 808-453-6055, Monday through Friday, 9:00 a.m. to noon
- Big Island: 808-322-4892, Thursdays, 9:00 a.m. to noon; 808-981-5199, Fridays, 9:00 a.m. to noon
- Maui: 808-244-3242
- Kaua'i: 808-274-3471, Monday through Friday, 8:00 a.m. to 4:30 p.m.

Water catchment

One of the best books on water catchment is free. "Guidelines on Rainwater Catchment Systems for Hawai'i" by Patricia Macomber of the University of Hawai'i is available online at ctahr.hawaii.edu/oc/freepubs/pdf/RM-12.pdf. It has careful rundowns on several common types of tanks and treatment systems, rainfall tables and a list of the Islands' water-borne diseases.

Food gardening resources

biochar-international.org/groups/hawaii
hawaiifruit.net
hawaiihomegrown.net
hawaiitropicalfruitgrowers.org
naturalfarminghawaii.net
sare.org—an excellent resource for sustainable agriculture

Tropical Horticulture

The University of Hawai'i's College of Tropical Agriculture and Human Resources website (ctahr.hawaii.edu/site/) is one of the most respected in the field of tropical horticulture. It has excellent information about food plants and ornamentals.

Nurseries

Locally owned nurseries have my highest recommendation. Not only do you get the best plants when you buy at locally owned nurseries; you also get the best advice.

O'ahu:
- David Yearian, 808-259-6322
- Frankie's Nursery, 808-259-8737
- Glenn's Flowers and Plants, 808-259-9625
- Hui Ku Maoli Ola, specializes in native plants, 808-235-6165
- Koba's Nursery, 808-259-5954
- Koolau Farmers, 808-247-3911
- Ladybug Plants, 808-259-8484
- Leilani Nursery, 808-259-9697
- N & S Nii Nursery, 808-395-9811
- Sharon's Plants, 808-259-7137

Big Island:
- Aikane Nursery, specializes in native plants, 808-889-5906
- Hawaiian Sunshine Nursery, 808-959-4088
- Paradise Plants, 808-935-4043
- Quindembo Bamboo Nursery, 808-885-4968
- Rozett's Nursery, 808-982-5422
- South Kona Nursery, 808-328-7338
- Special Ti Nursery, 808-966-7361
- Sunrise Nursery, 808-329-7593

Maui:
- Island Plant Company, 808-575-5094
- Ki Hana Nursery, 808-879-1165
- Maui Nui Botanical Gardens, 808-249-2798
- Native Hawaiian Tree Source, 808-572-6180
- Native Nursery, 808-878-8276
- Rainbow Acres Cactus and Succulent Nursery, 808-573-8318

Kaua'i:
- Garden Ponds Nursery, 808-828-6400
- Kauai Nursery and Landscaping, 808-241-5165
- Kauai Seascapes Nursery, 808-828-0444
- Kipapa Nursery, 808-639-1236

Moloka'i:
- Mahana Gardens, 808-567-6700

Index of Plant Lists

Not every plant on these lists will grow well where you live. Ask a landscape gardener, inquire at a nursery or call your local extension service. Let them know details like your average rainfall, elevation, proximity to the ocean and amount of shade. Hawaiʻi has many microclimates, and some plants that are invasive in one place are hard to grow a few miles away. Be a good neighbor and don't plant things that are invasive in your area. If in doubt, ask a knowledgeable plant person in your area, or consult the University of Hawaiʻi Weed Risk Assessment List: www.botany. Hawaiʻi.edu/faculty/daehler/wra/full_table.asp. This is the list of plants that have weed potential in Hawaiʻi. It is not definitive, and the site explains that another list is being compiled. My first choice to see if a plant has weed potential is *Permacopia* by Beyer and Martin. *See Recommended Reading, page 187.*

Index

Illustrations in italics

Main entries in bold

Acknowledgments

Steve Mann, Susan Levitt, Marisa Oshiro and Dawn Sakamoto were instrumental in making this book graceful and easy to understand.

Mahalo nui loa to those who allowed their gardens to be photographed or shared their knowledge: Amy Abe, Kimo Aipia, Lawton Allenby and Michael Katz, Leah and Charles Ashman, Brooke Marie Bacon, Linda Bong, Debra Bulosan, Norm Bezona, Ellen and James Bray, Bobbi Chinen, Clem Classen, Sana Daliva, Constance and Antonio Della Cioppa, Dianne and Jon Doherty, Diana Duff, Paul Endresen and Tom Sorensen, Teri and Rick Freeman, Randee Golden, Lucinda and Harold Goya, Una Greenaway, Stevie Heselton, Shelley and Paul Hoist, Hallie Iglehart, Carl Johnson, Barbara and Rob Kildow, Celah Kim, Margaret Krimm, Tai Lake, Judith Lau, Andrea and Brian Lievens, Maggie Liu, Ken Love, Joyce and David MacDonald, Chris McDonough, Conrad and Olamana Martel, Kathryn Miller, Michelle Morrison, Jiko and Michael Nakade, Kema Nash, Dennis Newkirk and Michael Wenger, Sherry Nicolson, Christy and John Ogg, Ira Ono, Emilia Parrish, Mary and Gary Radosky, Christine Reed, Patti and Paul Robinson, Getta and David Rogers, Christine Rolon, Grant Sairs, Michael Sisk, Louis Speilman, Jean Sunderland and Robert Watkins, Candice and Guido Tan, Sri TenCate, Martha Terao, Charles Umamoto, Jill Wagner, Deborah Ward and Fred Stone, Lydia and Roger Weiss, Duane Wenzel, Jonny Willing, Michael Winzman, Tina and Greg Wirth and Earl Yempuku. I also owe much appreciation to these businesses: Honua Landscaping, Kai Ea, Hale Lana, Hawai'i Island Retreat, Kohala Gardens Hideaway, Green Gecko Coffee, Tara Cottage Hawai'i, Tree Fern Cottage, South Kona Nursery, Special Ti Nursery, Horizon Guest House and Volcano Garden Arts.

Photo Credits

About the Author

Clear Englebert has taught feng shui in Hawai'i and California and consults on homes, gardens and commercial spaces throughout the Islands. His first bestselling book, *Feng Shui Demystified*, was originally published in 2000. It was followed the next year with *Bedroom Feng Shui*. The two books have appeared in four languages and, after a decade, have been reissued in revised and expanded editions. *Feng Shui for Hawai'i* is now in its third printing, also revised and with updated sources. His next book for a national market will be *Feng Shui for Retail Stores*. Upcoming Hawai'i titles *Interior Feng Shui in Hawai'i* and *Feng Shui Gardens in Hawai'i: An Elemental Balance* concern the use of the feng shui bagua. Visit www.fungshway.com.